Growing Up St. Louis

Looking Back Through the Decades

Jim Merkel

Reedy Press
PO Box 5131
St. Louis, MO 63139, USA

Library of Congress Control Number: 2019952734

ISBN: 9781681062549

Please visit us at jimmerkelthewriter.com
Facebook: Jim Merkel the Writer
www.reedypress.com

Cover and interior design by Claire Ford

Front cover images courtesy of: Cora (French) Katzen (top); State Historical Society of Missouri, Arthur Witman Collection. S0733_498 (bottom).

Printed in the United States of America

20 21 22 23 24 5 4 3 2 1

Growing Up St. Louis

Looking Back Through the Decades

Jim Merkel

Table of Contents

** This is one of seven first-person accounts of growing up in St. Louis from 1900 to 1919 taken from oral histories, books, and newspaper stories. All others in this book are from interviews with the author.*

Introduction

Before we were eight, when the grown ups towered above us, we lived in fairy tales. A jolly man in a red suit somehow delivered toys to millions of children around the world. A chair tipped over on the floor became the perfect seat for a rocket ship. It's irrational, to be sure, but it exercises the imagination. Those a bit older, say, up to high school graduation, have a firmer grasp on reality, but not completely. They're practicing for life as independent adults. Either way, our memories of childhood and adolescence have a simplicity that our recollections of the time since can never have.

This book contains the recollections of more than one hundred St. Louisans recounting their experiences of growing up in St. Louis from 1900 to 2019. I interviewed all but seven of them. The stories of those seven, taken from books, newspapers, and oral histories, represent the period from 1900 to 1919. I placed information from a handful of the interviewees into the commentaries because they seemed to fit better there. That leaves one more, me, in the epilogue, to tell what it was like to be a kindergartner in Des Peres when that West County community still was part of the country.

The stories provide a remarkable mix of people from the last 120 years of the city's history. Here are males and females, black and white, rich and poor, the famous and the forgotten, grouped chronologically in ten time periods. The sections for each of those ten periods begins with commentaries meant to provide context. The characters' eventual positions in life include homeless people, a future TV sports personality, teachers, and police officers. In most cases, their only identification besides their names are birth years, meant to let the reader know when they grew up. I also included a few facts about each time period, where they were illuminating or just fun. This isn't a scientific study, and the various people quoted herein don't always match the demographics. But the stories do come close to the feel of what St. Louis kids went through during different times since the beginning of the twentieth century.

The tales within these pages are in the words of the people I interviewed because that's the best way to bring a story to life. Most are pretty much word for word, with editing to smoothly combine material from one part of a recording to another. A little less than a fourth were done without recording. In those cases, the first-person memories were reconstructed from notes that are accurate but not verbatim. I'm satisfied that they truthfully recount what the people I interviewed meant to say and the spirit behind them. As much as I could, I allowed my interviewees to check what I wrote.

If the stories related herein stir nostalgic thoughts, all the better. If they cause readers to think of their own experiences growing up, wonderful. But that's not the book's main purpose. Rather, it's to remind us that what happens to us as adults is largely the result of our experiences as children. I've included happy and sad memories, with the hope that those of us whose childhoods were joyous might empathize with those who grew up in pain.

A caution: not all the stories are accurate. Nobody can remember a story about something they experienced ten, thirty, fifty or seventy years ago perfectly. That's common sense, but it's also what psychologists and other researchers who study memory say.

Where possible, I've sought to verify the stories. I've rejected ones that make me feel uneasy. I'm sure some of the ones in this book aren't completely right. Nonetheless, the stories are accurate where it matters. They provide the ring of truth. And independent facts back up many of the stories. Colleen La Croix talked about hearing trains at night in her childhood South County home, and there indeed is a train track not far away. When Dorothy Hunter, who was born in 1907, talked about walking to the movies from her house, that likely happened. Indeed, not far from her home on Connecticut Street was a movie theater. I had distinct memories of

Harper Avenue in Webster Groves, where I lived before I was five. When I visited Harper Avenue not long ago, the street was close to the way I remembered it. The same goes for my recollection that we used to watch *Have Gun Will Travel* and *Gunsmoke* on the same night. Old newspaper listings showed one show followed the other on Sunday nights. That's part of what gives the stories the ring of truth. I heard unusual detail in the stories told about the Japanese attacks on Pearl Harbor, the Kennedy assassination, and 9/11. They have the ring of truth, but not completely. Experts in memory call them "flashbulb moments." People accurately recall the core event, but over time, their memories of associated events change.

But even the misremembered details or stories convey a truth. Even when they're wrong, they are part of a person's life story, how a person defines himself. I firmly remember sneaking into a quarry near my house in Des Peres and being yelled at by workers there. Even if I hadn't sneaked into that quarry and got yelled at, my parents had given me the freedom to wander around, and I liked to sneak into places, where I shouldn't have gone. Taken with the other facts of history, this book provides the feel of what it was like to be a child from the beginning of the twentieth century to the present. Sit back, then, enjoy these memories of growing up in St. Louis, and imagine what it would be like to be a kid again.

jured Girl Who Is Being Made
Happy With Christmas Gifts

MISS MARIE MOENTMANN.

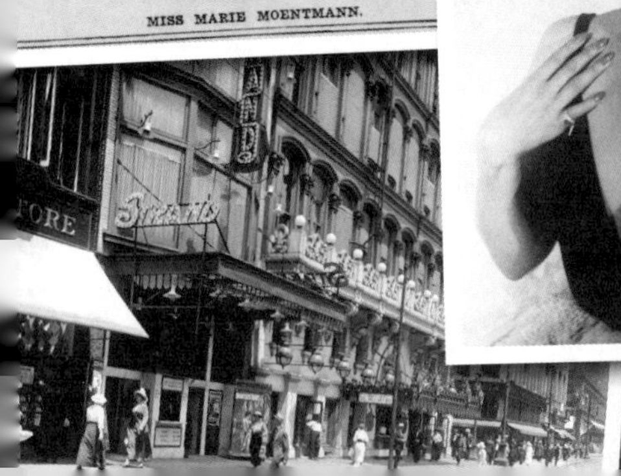

Hope for a New Century 1900–1919

The first two decades of the 1900s began with the hope that a new century would bring peace for all and wonders unimaginable. The energetic President Theodore Roosevelt battled trusts and fought to conserve monumental chunks of the American wilderness. But overseas today many see him as an imperialist. People got around on carriages without horses. Some even flew. But just when it seemed like things were getting better, Americans found themselves in a vicious world war, dampening their thought that the future would be better. And the country began an experiment in controlling behavior by outlawing liquor.

Locally, St. Louisans welcomed millions of visitors to the St. Louis World's Fair in 1904. The city thrived, as the fourth largest metropolis in the nation should. Progressives fought to improve lives for the poor through better housing, bathhouses, and playgrounds where kids could play in safety. But poverty and substandard housing persisted. By closing any place where people could gather and spread the local onslaught of the worldwide flu epidemic of 1918-19, Health Commissioner Dr. Max C. Starkloff kept the St. Louis death count reasonably low.

One particularly negative moment locally came when at least forty-eight people died and more than three hundred African American-owned businesses burned as enraged whites unleashed their anger on blacks in riots in East St. Louis in 1917. Whites who worried about losing their own jobs reacted angrily as more African Americans started moving from the South to northern industrial cities. St. Louisans voted in 1916 to keep people from buying a house in areas occupied by more than seventy-five percent of another race. The Supreme Court overturned it, but in many places homeowners signed papers promising they wouldn't sell to black people. Eventually the Supreme Court stepped in to void the covenants in 1948. The lack of livable wages meant that many African Americans in St. Louis were poor. But there were many business and professional people in segregated communities in the middle class. One who made better than the middle class wage was Annie Pope Malone, one of the first black women in the United States to become a millionaire. A chemist, she developed a line of beauty products specifically for black women. In 1918, she established Poro College, a cosmetology school that provided black women with training for well-paying jobs. The city's African American community also used it as a gathering place. She used most of her money to advance African Americans and to donate to charity, including the St. Louis Orphans Home, now the Annie Malone Children and Family Service Center. Thousands today turn out for the annual Annie Malone May Day Parade.

While grown-ups like Annie Malone worked, the kids played. The Fourth of July was a time to shoot off skyrockets and Roman candles and fly balloons. When Independence Day was a memory, kids turned out in force for that annual October rite, the Veiled Prophet Parade. Held in tandem with the hoity-toity Veiled Prophet Ball, the parade wound through downtown, where thousands watched. In 1915, the theme of the main float was "Myths and Legends." The favorite float that year was "Puss n Boots." That was kid stuff in comparison to the biggest children's holiday, Christmas. Often in the lead-up to the big day, parents and children would hop on streetcars for the trip downtown to shop at stores like Famous-Barr, the Broadway Store, and Schaper Brothers.

Holidays returned every year, but the greatest event of the era in St. Louis came only once: the Louisiana Purchase Exposition, known by many as the St. Louis World's Fair. Close to twenty million people stopped by the western edge of Forest Park in 1904 to see wonders unimaginable, like the mile-long Pike, the Tyrolean Alps, the Streets of Cairo, and an Eskimo Village.

A popular destination was the Philippine Reservation, a kind of zoo in which visitors could observe the lives of five different kinds of native peoples. Many remembered the Igorots, who were known for eating dogs. Today, most decry the display as an example of the degrading way indigenous people were exploited at the fair. Those who came to the St. Louis World's Fair told their kids and grandkids about their visits to the great Exposition. Those progeny might think the only thing that happened in the first two decades of the century was the World's Fair. It wasn't, but for kids of the time, it was easily the biggest thing.

Sixteen Times at the Fair*

Julia Davis, born 1891

Now the first day was the worst day of all for me, my first day at the Fair. We went into as many buildings as we could that our legs would carry us. We collected souvenirs all day—nails, tacks, anything. So here we come out with our two bags full of souvenirs, because I always brought home to mother, no matter where I went.

Yes, I was at the Fair—sixteen times, fifteen free days for public school children, and then on the sixteenth time you had to pay your fifty cents admission, but you'd get a free ride on that great big Ferris Wheel. Oh, that was the biggest thrill I ever had. To get on that Ferris Wheel and just ride. Now, to a thirteen-year-old girl, now you know what that was. I thought I was all over the world, when I was just right out here in the park.

The president of the United States visited the Fair. Well, you could see all the little school children, we all lined up there. The carriage stopped just about where my gang. . . . was all mixed, colored and white, it didn't make any difference. The deportment was beautiful of children. You didn't have fussing and fighting. We were so busy looking. And it was all the people of the world, too. They were all one. The carriage stopped right in front of where we were, and I just touched the carriage where the president was.

Julia Davis grew up to be a prominent local African American educator. She is the namesake of the Julia Davis Branch of the St. Louis Public Library.

Free Passes*

Willard B. Shelp, born 1891 or 1892

My name is Willard B. Shelp, and in the year 1904 I lived with my parents at 4313 Lindell Boulevard, and that was a very fortunate place to be because practically all of the activity in and around the Fair either started or finished on Lindell Boulevard.

One of my favorite things was the Boer War, which was held in an area which was covered with forest in those days, which was practically out toward Big Bend Boulevard. They had a great area there. They had real veterans from the Boer War in Africa and British soldiers, and they had cannons, and they conducted a regular war, and one of the highlights of the exhibition was a man, a British soldier on a horse, in a fort, and he was surrounded by the Boers, and he went up a ramp in the fort and jumped with the horse into a pond of water, and that was a great excitement for a twelve-year-old boy. That cost, I think, fifteen cents, and I didn't have fifteen cents very often, but whenever I did I went to the Boer War.

Favorite Toys

- Crayola crayons
- Raggedy Ann dolls
- Teddy bears
- Electric trains
- 3D viewers
- Kewpie dolls
- Ping pong
- Tinker toys
- Ouija boards
- Erector sets

Eating the Dogs*

Louise Schmidt Venverloh, born 1893

We were not allowed to see the Igorots. My mother and father went to see the Igorots, but my mother said, "Those people were not clothed. They only have loin-cloths on, and it isn't nice for children to see people who don't have clothes on." We could see them from a distance. They came upon one of the Igorot women cooking a pot of food, a great pot of food. She said, "What is that you're cooking?" And she said, "Rice and dog." They had a pen there where they had all their dogs. The city of St. Louis was very reluctant to let them have dogs. They ate dogs, so the city had to let them.

The Hereafter, we went in that. My aunt from Collinsville went in with her children. One was about nine years old at that time. The hereafter was beautiful. It was like heaven. Then, as you would walk along, all of a sudden you would see these flames and devils would come out from both sides, and they would rush right at you. I hung close to my mother. A cousin of mine, Eddy, he was so frightened. He was hysterical because that big red devil came out with horns and red satin suits, and those flames were like the red things they had on the Fourth of July—it lit up with flames and smoke.

Louise Schmidt Venverloh (center left) *and family ready to head for the World's Fair.*

A Very Young Bride*

Esther Whaley, born 1893 or 1894

In 1908, fourteen-year-old Esther Whaley came from Grafton, Illinois, to St. Louis with her fiancé to get married. Her husband-to-be, John Siddles, was forty.

Of course, I don't like to give up my playmates, but we were leaving our old home anyway, and I don't know any girls or boys in Grafton. And I don't like the long dresses, but Mother has been insisting on making my skirts long for some time because I grow so fast—but as far as being married, (in my mind) John has only changed from my big brother to my husband in my affections.

I have always known him, and I don't take any stock in any kind of love except the kind I have for my father and mother and brother, and that's the kind I have for John.

Nobody knows how long he has had this marrying notion in his head, but he didn't say a word about it until he was afraid I would go back to school and meet a lot of boys, silly boys, you know, and he is awfully jealous hearted.

School Days

St. Louis school-age population, 1901-1902

White: 159,921 **Black:** 8,416

Total enrollment in city public schools: 84,774

Estimated total enrollment in private and parochial schools: 30,000

Estimated number between six and twenty not enrolled in school: 53,563

Forty-Eighth Annual Report of the Board of Education of the City of St. Louis, Mo. for the Year Ending June 30, 1902

A Tragic Accident*

Marie Moentmann, born 1900 or 1901

Fifteen-year-old Marie Moentmann was constantly in the papers late in 1915, after she lost most of her arms after her hands were caught and crushed in a power cylinder press at the bag factory where she worked. A reporter interviewed her four years later, after the publicity died down.

If the accident which deprived me of my hands and part of my arms has resulted in throwing all the safety devices possible around the dangerous machinery in factories which employ boys and girls, and has brought about the passage of just compensation laws for the care of those maimed for life in such employment, then I am happy that my misfortunes have accomplished some benefit for others.

I have become so accustomed to these (artificial) hands and arms that I just go ahead and do the best I can. At first, it was hard, very hard, to help myself much, but I have made much progress since. There are many things I can do without asking for help, but there are others in which I find myself calling for aid. I have little trouble dressing, but it is difficult when it comes to fixing my hair.

Before I was hurt, I was right-handed, but now I guess I am a lefty. You see, the doctors left me a much larger part of my left arm than they did of the right, and as I get the benefit of more muscular power by reason of having that elbow, I quite naturally make more use of it.

At the typewriter, I do just fine. I have never done any copying work for pay, but I would not be afraid to try it if my customers were not in too much of a hurry for their finished work. If it were a speed contest, I would be beaten before the start.

Burned Feet*

Emily Hahn, author, born 1905

St. Louis was a hell of a place for a summer resort. It rests in a topographic hollow, and the air is unusually quiet, except for the times when everything blows up all at once in a cyclone. Our cyclones and tornadoes were inconvenient, and even dangerous, but we were proud of them.

Late in May, it would begin to heat up. Then we were permitted to go barefoot, outside of school hours—a privilege I did not appreciate, for the sidewalks burned my feet and the asphalt in the streets melted to a mushy consistency, streaking my legs with tar.

Wherever potholes in a street were being mended, there was a little heap of soft tar nearby, and I remember—though I hate to think about it—that we filched little pieces of the tar and chewed it. The parched grass of Fountain Park was easier than asphalt on the feet, but if one simply had to stay outside, the backyard was best. There we could turn on the garden hose and wallow. When the classroom thermometer at our school rose to about ninety, we were sent home.

The Shoe Named after a Comic Strip

Two years after Richard Outcault started a comic strip called "Buster Brown," the Brown Shoe Company of St. Louis introduced the Buster Brown shoe at the 1904 St. Louis World's Fair.

A Night of Terror*

Josephine Baker, born 1906

The year was 1917, the place St. Louis, Missouri. I was eleven and lay sleeping in the one-room shack my family called home.

Suddenly, Mama shook me awake.

Throwing back the threadbare patchwork quilt that covered the bed I shared with my brother and sisters, she pulled us to our feet. An ominous humming sound filled the air. It seemed to be drawing nearer. "Is there a storm coming, Mama?" my brother Richard asked. "No, not a storm, child. It's the whites. Hurry." I hurried along behind Mama, who had picked up little Willie May and was pushing Richard and my sister Margaret out the door.

"A white woman was raped," someone shouted, and although I didn't understand the meaning of his words, I knew that they described the ultimate catastrophe. The flames drew nearer. As the choking stench of ashes filled the air, I was overcome with panic. Mama threw us to the ground and covered us with her body. Nearby, a white man, his face contorted with hatred, was savagely beating a figure kneeling before him with what looked like a club. Finally he crumpled into the mud like a filthy scarlet rag. Mama quickly turned my face away.

Josephine Baker

A Pack of Chewing Gum

Dorothy (Danner) Hunter, born 1907

The first thing I remember was when we moved to Connecticut Street from McDonald or McKee. I'm not sure. It was a bigger house, two blocks south of Tower Grove Park. We had three floors. I remember people carrying blankets walking past, close to where I was living, to Tower Grove Park to sleep all night. I always played tennis, and I always played with boys. They were the only ones that got up early when I went up to walk to Tower Grove Park to play tennis. The boys had bikes. That's because I was a girl. I couldn't have a bike.

I was in trouble a lot at school. (laughs) I think I pulled on a girl's skirt as we were lined up to come in from recess. Something minor, but nothing was minor then. I belonged to the Ukulele Club at Cleveland High School. I was the leader. It was popular at that time. And I played the piano. I had piano lessons. I sang in the choir at the Union Avenue Methodist Church. The kind of movies that we went to were approved by my father. I liked mysteries. There was a movie house on Grand Avenue. We lived one block, a long, long block from Grand Avenue. We probably went on a Saturday because we weren't in school. I remember my uncle being down at Union Station. My father did not permit chewing gum. That was a no-no in our family. But when we went down to the station to see my uncle off to World War I, my uncle gave us each a package of chewing gum. A whole package, and we were in seventh heaven, and there wasn't a thing my father could say, because this was a gift from a man who was almost at war.

My chores were to scrub the front porch on Saturday, front porch and steps. I didn't date. My sister was beautiful, and from kindergarten on, there was always a boy walking her home. She did have a cluster of boys.

Dorothy (Danner) Hunter (left) *with siblings.*

It was either take the streetcar or walk. There was one car on Arsenal Street and one on Grand. I walked to the streetcar. One time I walked on the street car, and that was when I had passes up to a certain age, and the conductor refused to take my ticket because he thought I was too old. I wasn't too old. I was just tall. Then I got off the car and got on the next car.

Christmas Eve was spent with my grandparents, my maternal grandparents, Christmas Day at home. Candles weren't permitted. They were too dangerous. Gifts were mostly clothes. I think children obeyed more then than now.

If I had to use one word about the way we were brought up, what my father believed in, it was moderation.

Movie Houses Everywhere

In 1914, the City License Collector's Office said there were more than 150 neighborhood theaters in St. Louis. It matched a trend throughout the nation, in which about a third of the population watched movies each week around 1910 and half the population by 1920.

Melvin Theatre

Virginia Theatre

New Grand Centre Theatre

Tower Theatre

Shenandoah Theater

Ritz Theatre

The Orpheum

ILED PROPHET
Spirit of St.Louis
PEVELY DAIRY Co.
GRAND & CHOUTEAU
500
BABY FIRST
INTERNATIONAL AIR RAC
October 1, 2, 3. 1923

Between the War and the Crash 1920–1929

After the horror of the War to End All Wars, the country let loose in the Roaring Twenties. Women started the decade with a new right to vote. President Calvin Coolidge was known as a man of few words and a pro-business philosophy that benefited many but left a sizable number behind. Everybody looked to cash in on the stock market, at least until 1929. Jazz added to the frenzy of the century's third decade, with such songs as "The St. Louis Blues" and musicians like Jelly Roll Morton, King Oliver, and Louis Armstrong. Flappers in loose dresses and short hair showed the decade's wild spirit in speakeasies where people drank booze made illegal by Prohibition. Gangsters rushed to fill the demand for the forbidden elixir.

Locally, voters caught the spirit of the high-flying decade in a 1923 election when they overwhelmingly approved twenty of twenty-one bond issue proposals that totaled $87.4 million—nearly $1.3 billion in 2019 money. The bonds paid for improvements that still benefit the area, including the Soldiers Memorial, flood work on the River des Peres, and upgrades for streets throughout the city. Four years later, St. Louis businessmen bankrolled Charles Lindbergh's chancy flight across the Atlantic, and local kids greeted him loudly when he returned less than a month after he landed in Paris on May 21, 1927. As Lindbergh approached St. Louis on June 17, kids waited on the Mississippi River levee for him to arrive in his plane, the *Spirit of St. Louis.* Lindbergh zoomed over the excited youngsters, scooted under the Eads Bridge, and soared westward toward Lambert Airport, where twelve thousand people waited to greet him. The next day, parents and kids wanting a glimpse of history jammed a winding parade route in Lindbergh's honor from Forest Park to downtown. Around Lindell and Grand, three Boy Scouts approached his car to present him with memorabilia declaring he was an honorary member of the city's Troop No. 2. One, Joseph Ehrhardt, gave him a knife that read: "To Scout Lindy." The boy told Lindbergh, "I hope you don't cut yourself."

That joyous visit happened the same year as another, more tragic visitation. On September 1, 1927, a deadly tornado touched down near Manchester Avenue and Kingshighway Boulevard and roared northeast into Illinois. At Central High School, a tower crashed into the auditorium, next to a cafeteria filled with students. Rescuers digging through what had been a biology lab found the bodies of five girls. At West Belle School, a wall collapsed, killing an eleven-year-old girl. Altogether, the twister killed seventy-eight and seriously injured five hundred and fifty. Those who barely escaped death included Mrs. Anthony Lopez and her five children. As the twister neared, she sensed a distinct cast in the sky, like an earlier St. Louis tornado she survived in 1896. She rushed her children into a rear room on the seventh floor. As they clung to her, she decided they'd have a better chance in the next room. But she couldn't open the door. Then they heard a crash. The door gave way, and they saw both walls had tumbled in. The room she'd tried to enter was in ruins.

The same year as the tornado, the city's Board of Education opened a second school for "colored" high school students. The school was a victory for local African Americans who long had pressed for another school to handle a sharp increase in the number of black students. Sumner, the city's only high school for African Americans, had been hopelessly overcrowded. Black enrollment in the city schools still was only thirteen percent of the whole at the decade's end, but more growth was ahead. The namesakes of the second high school for African Americans were George Vashon, a lawyer and the first African American graduate of Oberlin College in Ohio and his son John Vashon, a longtime city educator. There were recognizable African American communities with professionals and merchants. For example, Louise Jimerson, who was born in 1917, recalled that her home town of Madison, Illinois, had numerous grocery stores and churches.

Whatever their station in life, parents of the 1920s loved to lavish their kids with as much of the fun things as they could afford. Moms and dads thrilled their offspring with mighty quantities of cheap toys from Japan and Germany, along with Tinker Toys and Lincoln Logs. They cheered when the Cardinals beat the Yankees to win their first World Series in 1926. Radio brought voices and music from afar into living rooms. On October 3, 1922, KSD broadcast the sound of His Majesty's arrival from the Mythical Kingdom of Khorassan in the annual Veiled Prophet Parade downtown. By 1926, ten stations were on the air, many with new programs for kids.

People thought the good times would go on forever, but disaster was ahead. On Black Tuesday, October 29, 1929, investors lost billions, ending the decade's wild prosperity. At Christmas, many believed the crash was a temporary reversal. Surveys showed Americans were buying more gifts and sending more cards than ever. About twenty-five thousand Missouri Pacific Railroad employees and their families watched as Santa arrived in the Arena, ready to give out about ten thousand children's packages. It may have been the largest Christmas party in the city, but it was hardly the only one. But ominous signs portended change. On Christmas Day 1929, the *St. Louis Star* headlined that Mayor Victor Miller was considering suggestions that he convene a conference of financial and business leaders to deal with rising city unemployment. Soon, many more would find themselves without work. Hard times were ahead, especially for kids.

A High School Degree

Margaret (Thurston) Whitaker, born 1913, retired schoolteacher

Since Margaret Whitaker's family lived west of Kirkwood, her father would be forced to pay for her to go to high school. But he didn't want her to go to high school.

I did it myself since I wanted to go. I always wanted to be a teacher, and that meant I was going to high school. First, I had to talk to the superintendent of schools, and he told me that I should go to Kirkwood and live with this woman as a maid and take care of her and look after her. She worked for the *Countian* newspaper, and I lived with her for five years while I finished high school. Since her house was right near the school, I could walk there.

My mother was a beautiful lady and my dad was very fortunate to have her. She raised me to be a Christian. She was a Seventh Day Baptist, meaning she wasn't Jewish, but she believed in the seventh day as the Sabbath. I went with her to church when I was little. It was right on our block and it was open all the time. I'd go in and pray and sing, and then I'd go and play around on the piano with one finger.

Top Destinations for Kids

Forest Park

The Zoo

Forest Park Highlands

Creve Coeur Lake

Lighting the Streets

Helen Arbogast, born 1914

We had gaslights outside for streetlights. Every evening about dusk, a man would come through and use something on a stick and turn them on. It was our light throughout the night. In the morning, he'd come through and turn them off.

We had a lot of fun riding the streetcars. They had a motor man and a conductor. You would get on at the back, and right there was a conductor where you had to pay your fare, and when all the people were on, he would pull the chain, and that would tell the motor man to start.

My dad worked for this one company that made the Veiled Prophet floats. They had a unique way of lighting up the floats. One man would walk down the street behind the floats holding a stick with a bar across the top. If he held the bar up across the wire that powered the streetcars, the electricity would light the float. If the float went too fast, he had to hurry to keep up. The line of floats went down the street, and he kept up.

Do's and Don'ts

Drink a pint to a quart of milk every day. Eat meats but once daily. Eat candies, cake, etc. only as directed.

Do not eat candies, cakes, or ice cream between meals.

Sleep with windows open every night.

Keep fingers out of mouth. Do not bite.

Do not put corners of books in the mouth.

Do not dampen fingers in the mouth to turn the pages of a book.

Take a full tub bath twice every week. Sponge the arms and chest daily in cold water. Wash perspiring feet every day.

Sixty-Seventh Annual Report of the St. Louis Board of Education, for the Year Ending June 30, 1921

At Home with a Doctor and His Wife

Erna Gehle, born 1914

My family was so poor that instead of going to high school I had to go to work in a private home with good people, a doctor and his wife, in St. Louis. My parents didn't go with me. I went by myself. I did the cleaning, the cooking, the laundry. I did everything. I cleaned on my hands and knees, although they did at least have a vacuum cleaner.

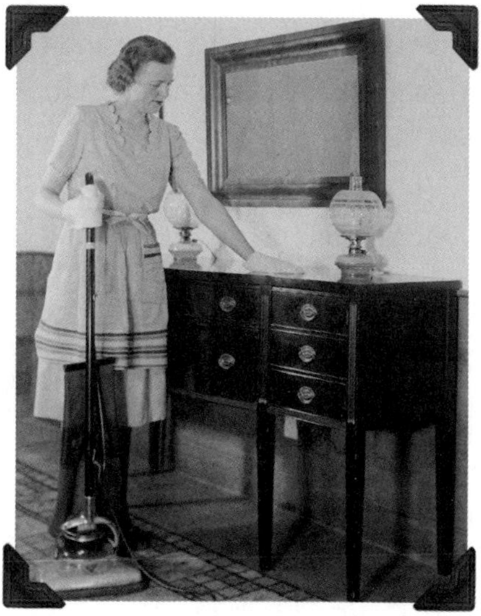

It was so different there, in those years, from what I had grown up with. On the farm, we had horses, cows, sheep, ducks, chickens. I went back to the farm just for summer vacations. The doctor and his wife took me in like one of the family. Well, not exactly, but they were good to me, and took me with them a lot when they were with their family. I had a nice sized room, my own bed and everything, and the house had eight rooms in all. Nowadays it really would be scary to leave your home and work for other people, but they got me started here in St. Louis. I worked until I went to night school, and then I took up bookkeeping.

Mounds of Cobbler

Louise Jimerson, born 1917

We used to have fourteen grocery stores here during my childhood, grocery stores on every corner. I remember chicken neck bones were three pounds for twenty-five cents, and Wonder Bread was five cents a loaf. We got candy and pickles and gum. I remember my mother used to cook a lot of potatoes. My grandmother used to bake some cookies for us, sugar cookies, we called them. My grandmother and my mother would cook Sunday dinner, and we'd have fried chicken, mashed potatoes, peas, potato pie, pecan pie, apple cobbler, peach cobbler, cherry cobbler. My grandmother and my mother always would can fruit in the fall. They made them into preserves: strawberry preserves, peach preserves, blackberry preserves.

My dad was the custodian at Dunbar School in Madison, Illinois, for thirty years, and my mother was a homemaker. It was my grandmother who lived with us who did the disciplining. She always would spank me. Next door to me was my uncle. He'd always be over at our place. It seems like we'd always have seven or eight people there.

I went to visit one of my aunts in Memphis when I was thirteen years old. She told me how to get to downtown in Memphis on the streetcar. There weren't buses then I remember sitting on the front row behind the conductor, and the conductor looked back to me. He said, "Girlee"—he called me "Girlee"—"Where are you from, New York?" And I told him, no, I was from St. Louis. And he told me, "Next time you get on this street car, you go back as far as the whites stop on the street car." When I got off, he said "You remember what I told you."

Almost an Orphan

Madelyn (Pedrotti) Gaasch, born 1917

Madelyn Gaasch

My mother? She was a good lady, a hard-working lady, and my father was a nice, good man, too, at least the way I remember him. I do not have bad feeling for him. Then he met this lady, and you know how ladies can be. He was with her and she was not going to accept just living with somebody. She wanted marriage, and that's what she insisted on. So he asked my mother for a divorce, but she did not want it. And so he left her, which was awful—I don't even like to tell the story.

Then I woke up one morning, and my mother was gone, too. They took her to the hospital, but it was too late. I was just eight years old when she died. My brother, who was eighteen or nineteen at the time, stuck with me and stayed with me until I got a home, and then he left. I had heard that he lived in California for a while, but I've never seen him since. And that's hard, too; it's just sad to think about it.

After that, my uncle tried to get a home for me instead of putting me in an orphanage. Elsie and Charles Pedrotti took me from there. My mother had died, and I needed a home, and they didn't want to put me in an orphanage, so they raised me. They were very good parents. They sent me to Catholic school and had me baptized, first thing. I had a very good life with them, especially after losing the rest of my family.

He Lost His Marbles

Ed Hetzer, born 1917

We were a bunch of mischievous kids. On Halloween we used to go around and we would empty other people's trash cans out on their lawns. We were chased one time and we had to make a run for it. But my brother fell and twisted his knee, and the doctor said it was water on the knee.

We would go to the movies on Saturdays, which cost us ten cents to get in. Popcorn was another nickel extra so we didn't get the popcorn. Talkies, that was something new and exciting for us. Before, it was always just writing on the screen.

I used to play marbles with my thumb bent behind the second finger, because I could shoot really good that way. I never bought any marbles, just won all of them in the games. I ended up with a can so high, so big around, full of marbles I'd won. I wonder whatever happened to them.

Some top children's books of the 1920s

Winnie-the-Pooh

Emil and the Detectives

The Story of Dr. Doolittle

Emily of New Moon

The Milly Molly Mandy Storybook

Just William

What Do We Do All Day? Website

A Kiss without a Squeeze

Hortense "Blondie" (Bushman) Ott, born 1919

In those days, before people had refrigerators, the ice man would come around. He was one of many delivery men that came around the neighborhood. They'd put the ice in your ice box to cool your food because there was no such thing as a refrigerator. The Pevely Dairy man came by with a horse and wagon to deliver the milk. Then the produce man used to go by to sell produce. The White Bakery truck had a sign that read "An apple pie without cheese is like a kiss without a squeeze. But whether you have cheese or not, here's a pie that will knock you out."

Streetcars were all over St. Louis, and they used to have a streetcar that went all the way out to Creve Coeur Lake. In the summer, the cars on that line would be open cars so you could sit and enjoy the view—like park benches, almost. They had a streetcar line that went all the way out to St. Charles, too, but they had no place to turn around. So the cars were made so they could run back to town facing the other way.

A Smelly, Icky Old Out House

Elizabeth Louise (Fresenburg) Meyer, born 1921

When I was living on Beck Avenue, we had an outhouse just like all the other houses had at that time. Really I think it was more like a bench with a hole in it. It smelled bad all the time in there, a permanent smell that would just stay there. I think we did have potty chairs in the house, though, so that in the middle of the night we didn't have to go all the way outside to the outhouse. One time, the seat on the bench came loose and needed to be repaired—I was in danger of falling into the hole!

Cowboys on the Silver Screen

Yakima Canutt in *Captain Cowboy*

Hoot Gibson in *The Buckaroo Kid*

Tom Mix in *King Cowboy*

Bob Custer in *The Devil's Gulch*

Buck Jones in *The Circus Cowboy*

Neal Harl in *The Secret of the Pueblo*

Gary Cooper in *The Last Outlaw*

Alamy Cowboys 1920s Stock Photos, Vectors and Videos Website

One Proud American

Frank Fontana, born 1922

My dad's name was Jerome, and he came from Sicily. He came over probably in 1916, and stayed with his uncle. Then he was in World War I, on the American side, of course, and served in Europe on the front lines. He became a citizen automatically because he was in World War I. You might add, a very proud citizen, because he was. After his discharge, he went back to see his parents in Sicily and married my mother, Mary, whom he'd known since she was a little girl. They came back here to live on Franklin Avenue—at 18th and Franklin.

My dad never could get a good job, and my parents had no money. Nothing. But nobody else ever had anything, either. Finally he went to work at Stix Baer & Fuller on the night cleanup crew. Then he became the ice cream maker at Stix Baer & Fuller's restaurant. My mother was a seamstress at a garment factory at Washington and 11th with all Jewish and Italian ladies. They spoke three languages in the shop: English, Italian, and Yiddish. From second grade to graduation, I went to St. Liborius Catholic grade school run by the Notre Dame Sisters. They were strict, but I was a very good student. So good that I could read a catechism in German by the time I was in second grade. The neighborhood and the school were mostly German, followed by Irish, and then not many Italians.

the
WAR
Against
DEPRESSION
YOU
AND
Give
a
Man
a
Job
We'll WIN!

Hitting Bottom
1930–1939

In the 1930s, the middle class learned what it was like to be poor. The poor learned destitution. Those who worked made less, but fewer worked. President Herbert Hoover's answer to the Great Depression was to ask companies to maintain salaries and unions to stop demanding raises. It didn't work. By 1933, one worker in four was unemployed. So voters elected a new president who promised a New Deal for America. Franklin Roosevelt pushed through a long list of reform bills that permanently changed the country. They helped farmers, sought to reduce the chance of bank failure, protected senior citizens through Social Security, supported unions, and put the unemployed to work.

Times were bad everywhere, but they were worse in St. Louis, where one worker in three was unemployed at the worst point. The city borrowed millions for relief and slashed salaries and the city's budget. Federal money created work for cleaning streets and creating rock slopes on the River des Peres. The project that led to the building of the Gateway Arch started in part as a plan to put thousands to work building a riverfront memorial to President Thomas Jefferson and the westward expansion.

Civic renewal projects eased unemployment, but destitution persisted throughout the decade, particularly along the riverfront south of downtown. The place was one of many settlements called Hooverville, after President Herbert Hoover. The cardboard, driftwood, and crates that made up shacks in the settlement did little more than keep off the rain, and then not always. The suffering of many African Americans exceeded that of the residents of Hooverville. Worse, some charitable organizations even excluded African Americans from soup kitchens. But even in the Depression, some African Americans saw improvements in their incomes.

Black doctors made good money working at the new Homer G. Phillips Hospital for African Americans in the Ville neighborhood. Real estate covenants that prevented African Americans from moving into white neighborhoods pushed those doctors and their families into places like the Ville, along with other prominent African Americans. The neighborhood became a cultural center for African Americans and the childhood home of Chuck Berry and opera star Grace Bumbry. Meanwhile, Mayor Bernard Dickmann said he'd get more jobs for African Americans in such positions as porters. But one black leader, Jordan Chambers, said he wanted better-paying jobs got African Americans in such positions as police officers. In the meantime, housing conditions for black people in St. Louis were deplorable. For many African Americans, any hope of a better life in the 1930s was out of reach.

The distress of many in the 1930s hints at how bad things were in the Depression, but what happened on an unseasonably warm January day in 1933 in North St. Louis shows the misery of the time. On that day, Joseph Lynch found a newborn infant girl in an ashpit behind his home on St. Louis Avenue. Doctors at City Hospital estimated the baby had been born a mere two hours before. Had the weather been more typical of January, the child might not have survived.

The Depression didn't spare children who saved their nickels and dimes in local banks through a program of the St. Louis Public Schools. Young savers joined their parents in losing everything when two of those banks closed. But the city's immigrant communities got through the Depression with help from each other. Greeks in St. Louis banded together to find work for the jobless and provide for the needy. Family members, including kids, brought in what money they could. When Greek immigrant Peter Tsichlis's grocery store closed, his seven kids pitched in. Eldest daughters Ann and Mary worked at movie theaters. Oldest son George worked at Butler Brothers clothing distributors. Sister Frieda left school to work in a dressmaker's shop. Twin brothers Sam and Angelo, about seven, sold magazines on the street with their brother Jimmy, about eleven. Together, they made enough to buy food and pay the $30 a month rent on their house.

The hardships, hunger, and adventure of growing up in the Depression were familiar to the writer A.E. Hotchner. In *King of the Hill*, his vivid memoir of life in the 1930s in St. Louis, he told what happened when a twelve-year-old boy and his parents lived in a bug-infested hotel at Delmar and Kingshighway Boulevards, always on the edge of eviction. The situation became especially grim when the boy was left alone to fend for himself after his mother entered a tuberculosis sanitarium and his father went on the road selling timepieces. To avoid eviction, he locked himself into his room. To keep hunger away, he cut pictures of sumptuous meals out of food articles in a magazine, placed them on a plate and ate them. As doom approached, his father returned to rescue him and inform him he had a steady job that would allow the family to move into a good house.

Hotchner's stories described how grim the Depression could be. But even in the worst of times, kids with radios still could listen to *The Lone Ranger* or *Little Orphan Annie*. Kids watched movies in palaces with names like the Kingsland or the Melba Theaters. The Cardinals in the 1930s thrilled the younger set with stars like Pepper Martin and the Dean brothers. They won the World Series in 1931 and 1934. Even better, they got into Cardinals or Browns games for free, through Knothole Gang passes for kids who showed good grades and good behavior. Kids whose parents had money could go swimming or on rides at the Forest Park Highlands or the Chain of Rocks Amusement Park. For those without cash, there were free pools in the city and parks.

The Depression was hard, but it led to a new social covenant. Legislation meant to guarantee people wouldn't starve established a willingness to accept help from the federal government that continues today. Whether in their frugality or their belief that they could get through anything, survivors of the Depression always said it helped form them for the rest of their lives.

Shunned

Vivian (Wides) Zwick, born 1917

I went to Clayton High School, and at first everybody was very nice to me. I was even asked to be a member of a sorority. But the next day, they came and told me that because I was Jewish, I couldn't be in their sorority. It was such a shock.

Later, Mother suggested that I go to University City High School, where I already had a lot of friends. That's how I wound up at University City High School. I liked it, and I was happy there. I had a lot of friends.

University City High School

Kids without Parents

1904	13.8
1933	20.8
1944	14.9

Number of kids in foster homes and institutions in St. Louis per 1,000 population

Run on the Bank

Louise Jimerson, born 1917

My grandmother raised a lot of chickens in her backyard during the Depression that she would sell for fifty cents apiece. During the Depression, we would head down to Hunter's Packing House in East St. Louis from Madison, Illinois, to get meat for the family. They would give out free meat there during the Depression. My dad lost all his money at Madison Bank. He went up one Monday morning to get some money, and they said the bank was closed.

Louise Jimerson in 2017

A Very Merry Christmas

In the depths of the Depression, the Mayor's Christmas Party was a party to end all parties. Democrat mayor Bernard Dickmann, elected in the spring of 1933, buttonholed businesses to dole out 15,000 bottles of soda, 12,000 pints of milk, 12,000 pounds of sweet potatoes, 3,000 gallons of coffee, and monumental amounts of other goodies in his holiday extravaganza on Christmas Day 1933. About 2,000 city employees served 26,773 meals in the Municipal Auditorium and Community Center at Market and 14th streets, now the Stifel Theater and the Enterprise Center.

Three Brown Cows

Frank Fontana, born 1922

At the end of school in June when I was twelve or thirteen, we would go to the library downtown and get a Knot Hole Gang pass—a season's pass to see the Browns and the Cardinals. We could go to every ball game except those on Saturday and Sunday. We could go to a hundred games if we wanted. You want to hear some prominent names of the players we saw? Pepper Martin. Then it was Joe Medwick and Dizzy and Paul Dean. We didn't get to see the stars much, though, because they always pitched on Sundays. The Browns were terrible at that time, but we didn't care.

We'd walk to the games even though it was a forty-five-minute walk. You see, our parents would give us fifteen cents each because we needed a nickel to get there on the streetcar, a nickel to get back, and a nickel for an ice cream bar. But we were smart, so we'd walk and save the streetcar nickels so we could get three ice cream bars instead. They called them Brown Cows and we polished off a lot of them when we went to all those games during the summer at Sportsman's Park.

Kiddie radio programs

Dick Tracy	*Tom Mix*	*Buck Rogers*
The Green Hornet	*Tarzan*	*Howdy Doody Time*
	Flash Gordon	*Challenge of the Yukon*

Old Time Radio Catalog website, Children's Radio Shows.

Smoke Downtown

Marjorie (Jones) Raker, born 1923

In the 1930s, sooty, high-sulfur coal from Southern Illinois that powered St. Louis's furnaces, factories, and trains darkened the daytime sky and covered everything with a dark dust.

Marjorie (Jones) Raker

Going to St. Louis from De Soto was a three-hour trip, and occasionally we did have to come to St. Louis on a shopping trip. I remember being at Famous Barr downtown, coming out the Seventh Street side and not being able to see the Forum Cafeteria across the street because of all the smoke. When we got home to De Soto after one of those shopping trips, we wiped our faces with a Kleenex, and it was black with smoke. I knew people in De Soto who had moved away from St. Louis to escape the smoke for their health.

I never had to worry about where my next meal was coming from, but I know there were people in my class at school who did. I remember people coming to our house for food. They were never turned down. They would sit on my back steps and eat a sandwich. World War II and the Great Depression were the defining events of my lifetime and my husband's family.

The Train to Arkansas

Dorothy McFerren, born 1925

I liked traveling. I really did, and I loved to go down south. I would always get to go on vacation to Arkansas. I must have been about ten when I first went down there. My grandmother and grandfather were down in Wynne, Arkansas, in the country and we had a lot of relatives there who lived in town. We didn't have to do anything on the farm. They had cotton down there, but they wouldn't let me pick it. My brothers went several times, too. One time my oldest brother broke his leg when he jumped off a barn.

We took the train down south, and on some of the trains, you had to sit separate. That's one of the reasons my brothers didn't like to go down there: the segregation. We had to act different. We didn't understand why we had to say "Yes ma'am" and "No, ma'am." My brothers said, "I don't want to go to Arkansas, Momma. Do we have to go?" "Yep," she'd say. In the end, I didn't care myself about the differences at the time, since I was just a kid.

Groceries from Roosevelt

Jennie (Patania) Crittenden, born 1925

I don't know if anyone ever gave us any clothing, but I remember having very bad shoes with cardboard in them. My mother used to get cardboard so I could keep my feet on the ground.

We always had pretty good food, though. You see, when Franklin Roosevelt was president, my mother used to get baskets of groceries that were brought to my home. And she used to get credit from the grocery store so she could make dishes that I don't even do now, like veal cutlets and rabbit and ravioli. We'd have to do them by hand with a rolling pin, grind the meat. It was a lot of work, but very delicious, and we'd have relatives once in a while from New York. For them, we'd set out a big table spread of delicious Italian food.

President Franklin Roosevelt

How Bad Was It?

The number of unemployed skyrocketed from about 1.5 million in 1929 to nearly 13 million in 1933.

Bowls of Ralston

William H. Danforth, born 1926, Chancellor Emeritus, Washington University

My grandfather was the founder of Ralston Purina Co., which used to make cereal and other packaged foods in addition to pet food. He grew up in Charleston, Missouri, and came to St. Louis to finish his education. He was a model citizen for his eight grandchildren. We started in an apartment in St. Louis and moved to a house in Clayton. It was a large stone house built about 1928. There were four of us in all, and my younger brother Jack became a senator. He always wanted to go into politics. Our middle brother Don Jr. would practice interviewing Jack and try to think up hard questions to ask him.

We ate Ralston whole wheat cereal every morning for breakfast; after all, it was the family business. When we went to Ralston Purina, there was milling going on there. It had a wonderful smell. I saw Tom Mix down there and Admiral Byrd. Tom Mix was a famous cowboy who had been in the movies, and then he became the hero of a children's daytime serial sponsored by Ralston Purina. He was brave, courageous and fought for law and order. The show was built around the character Tom Mix. The kids in it were Jane and Jimmy.

A Sandwich for Lunch

Elizabeth June Harper, born 1926

Elizabeth June Harper

We lived right at Oakland and Kingshighway on Arco Avenue, right behind St. Louis University High School. The Depression was hard because money was very tight, and we were pretty poor. By trade, Dad was a butcher, but to make ends meet he just did odd jobs. He did a little tree work, or he did some painting. He was very good at carpentry work. He was very talented in whatever he set out to do; it seemed like he could do anything. Mother took in washing and ironing for a while. Later on, she worked for Sears and Roebuck on Kingshighway.

A lot of men wanted odd jobs around the house, and my mother would give them a sandwich or something. We always had a little garden in the back, and she was generous. She would make them a sandwich.

We heard they were giving shoes out to the people that needed them, so somebody took us downtown and got us a pair of shoes. Instead of coming to a point or rounded at the toe, they came straight across. Oh, like a box. Ugly brown. I hated them, but I had to wear them.

Everybody in our neighborhood lived like the "Scrubby Dutch," which meant we kept our houses scrubbed sparkling clean. I scoured the outside of our house many times, always the steps. We used Comet or whatever they had then. We scrubbed those concrete steps so clean, and we used to think it was fun. You didn't dare walk up on the steps if your shoes were dirty.

Growing Up Catholic

Mary Schuette, born 1926

I was born in South St. Louis, but I lived in the county all my life. I went to grade school at St. George in Affton. We had big classes, and I remember having a nun and a lay teacher as assistant, and they were strict, but that's what we needed. It wasn't learning like they do now. It wasn't just play. They taught us religion and how to treat people. They didn't beat us over the head, but they were preparing you for life and for school. I can remember the excitement of being able to see Jesus for the first time in First Communion.

We didn't have anything during the Depression but thank goodness, my dad still had his job. I would get my two sisters' clothes; back then a lot of clothes were hand-me-downs. For fun, we listened to mysteries on the radio, but we couldn't have it on during homework time.

Life Without Dad

Ralph Naslund, born 1926

My mother worked as a bookkeeper. My father died of tuberculosis that he contracted in World War I. And when he died, she received a pension. It was $40. How about that? If you lived in the height of the Depression, you lived hand to mouth. Unless you lived in that era, it was difficult to comprehend. I sold newspapers. I had a magazine route, *Liberty* and *True Story*. The ladies were quick with a nickel and dime for *Liberty* and *True Story*.

The big deal was on Sunday; we could buy a Sunday pass for ten cents and you could ride the streetcar all day. One of my highlight trips was coming out to Kirkwood. Or we would ride the Delmar Line to Creve Coeur Lake. My cousin and I would ride, four or five of us would ride out together. After a good Saturday night selling newspapers, we could ride over to the East Side.

A Red Wagon

Sidney Duerr, born 1927

When times got hard, nobody would buy anything in hardware stores, so my dad lost his hardware store in Old Orchard in Webster Groves. He moved all of his stuff into the basement. My job was to go get the lawn mowers and bring it to him to sharpen. After he lost the store, my dad got a job at a hat company. During the Depression, my mother took care of three old ladies. The neighbors behind us, they were really poor, and we kind of helped them, too. That's how we got through, everybody helping out. There weren't any politics.

On my fifth birthday, August 6, 1932, I got a beautiful red wagon. I rode the wagon down Tuxedo onto Laclede Station Road, where a big truck carrying rocks ran over me. A doctor was behind me and brought me to the hospital. All the while, I was crying because my red wagon was gone.

Sidney Duerr pulls his little brother, Donald.

PLANT A VICTORY GARDEN
OUR FOOD IS FIGHTING
A GARDEN WILL MAKE YOUR RATIONS GO FURTHER

DRINK Coca-Cola

From Rations to Plenty 1940–1949

Technically, the 1940s were a single decade. But the wartime first half of the 1940s was a world away from the peacetime second half. The nation and its kids changed radically with the attack on Pearl Harbor on December 7, 1941, and just as radical when the atomic bomb ended the war in 1945. In the early years, men shipped out to fight, leaving the home front to the women who remained. When they returned after the war, men would find many of the women unwilling to leave their jobs. Russians replaced Nazis as enemies. The number of marriages and births skyrocketed. An unprecedented era of prosperity started in America.

In the decade's first half, people in St. Louis worked to defeat their foes in two hemispheres. That work sometimes came with pain or long-term harm. Mayor William Dee Becker, two crew members, and seven other local leaders died in the crash of a military glider on August 1, 1943, at what was then called Lambert-St. Louis Municipal Airport. Ten thousand people watched as the glider slammed into the ground. A local company, Mallinckrodt Chemical Works, processed uranium downtown for the first atomic bomb. Radioactive waste the company stored in north St. Louis County eventually leaked out, contaminating lawns and food sources and causing cancers among local residents.

During the war, children couldn't fight, but they could plant a victory garden, collect rubber or metal for recycling, give their coins toward a war bond, or put their all into a song at a rally. Rationing of red meat, butter, and other items meant children and adults couldn't always eat their favorite meals. God-awful oleomargarine took the place of butter. Kids hankering for metal toys and bisque dolls under the tree had to settle for imitations made of wood, plastic, and fabric.

Thankfully, the conflict didn't last forever. Young families searching for open spaces started moving out of St. Louis to previously empty places, like Oakville, Florissant, or Affton. A new generation came that was different from those before it. The *News of*

St. Louis Hills demonstrated how parents of the time doted on their kids. The slick monthly promo magazine offered the latest details about teas, gossip, and new homes of Cyrus Crane Willmore's St. Louis Hills subdivision. It was a rare cover that didn't feature cute youngsters drinking sodas at a fountain, swimming, posing in the arms of Santa, or riding a tricycle.

With the end of the war, the battle against segregation speeded up. Protests over white-only department stores, schools, and lunch counters grabbed headlines. Archbishop Joseph E. Ritter integrated Catholic schools. City pools were integrated, but on the first day of the new policy, white teenagers armed with baseball bats, bricks, and pipes attacked black youth who showed up to swim at the Fairground Park pool. The Supreme Court ruled in 1948 that real estate covenants barring African Americans from buying a house in certain St. Louis neighborhoods were unconstitutional. When the war ended, GIs came home to St. Louis and started trends that continue today. Many families and businesses moved. Some African American veterans started getting jobs with decent wages. A few moved into the middle class. Many of the area's African Americans found refuge from racism in all-black enclaves like North Webster. There were movies on Wednesday nights at the volunteer fire house. There was a country club, several grocery stores, doctors, taverns, and a restaurant.

Wherever kids lived, they rushed to the movies or to Sportsman's Park to see the Cardinals and the Browns games with special free tickets. The Cardinals trounced the Browns in the '44 World Series, just as they crushed the Yankees in the '42 series and the Red Sox in the '46 series. Even when the Cards weren't in the pennant race, Stan Musial, Red Schoendienst, and Enos Slaughter dazzled. Kids could listen to games on the radio, or to Gene Autry on KMOX, or Sherlock Holmes on KWK. When KSD-TV went on the air in 1947, kids could watch games at home, but only if their parents could afford a television set.

Soon, television would dominate the lives of children and adults, but at Christmas in the 1940s, toys provided the entertainment. Wartime rationing had stopped the use of steel for toys, but it was back after the conflict. For about $36, mom and dad could put a Gilbert American Flyer Electric AC Train Set next to the tree. Parents delighted in giving their kids a better life. For decades after, kids would be the center of life in America.

Love at Woolworth's

Elizabeth June Harper, born 1926

I started a job at Woolworth's when I was almost sixteen. It was a big store at Grand and Olive. I worked on a little counter that sold shoestrings and stuff like that, and I loved it. I even met my husband there. He was a stock boy and I thought he was pretty cute. His father was a Woolworth's manager. The store had a big soda fountain where you could get anything you wanted: food or sodas. He used to bring me one and then hide it at the counter—usually a Coke, a small Coke, I think. On the side of the glass, it read "Coca-Cola."

Listening to Roosevelt

William H. Danforth, born 1926, Chancellor Emeritus, Washington University

I was in high school at St. Louis Country Day School when war was declared. I went to school on Monday and they brought all the students together to hear Roosevelt's speech.

President Franklin Roosevelt

Kids' movies

Pinocchio

Dumbo

Miracle on 34th Street

Song of the South

Son of Lassie

Getting the News Out

James Conway, born 1932, St. Louis Mayor 1977-1981

James Conway

I was selling newspapers as a child when World War II broke out. I recall everyone was out on their front porch with their porch lights on. The next day I was back on my route and everyone wanted a newspaper. We were sold out in no time. You have to appreciate I was nine years old, so I cannot exactly remember when I heard about the war or the instant I heard about it, but it was one of those things that was just overwhelming and people wanted to comprehend as much as they could.

I was the oldest of seven children. During the war, my father was called up twice for the draft, but they wouldn't take him because of his family responsibilities. My father was an auto worker and he was very involved in the organization of United Autoworkers Local 25, working for the Fischer Body Division of General Motors, and oftentimes the company had strikes and model changes. The employees would be laid off while they refitted the plant for new models. Things were generally tough.

I cannot ever recall us being poor, but my father and his brother-in-law, who also worked for General Motors, were avid hunters and fishermen. That was a source of food at times. The union itself would supply various meats and vegetables. It was a difficult time for everyone. I did not feel it personally, but you don't realize how things are when you're a small child. It meant that to have any kind of spending money, I had to earn it. Ever since I was "knee high to a grasshopper," I've done everything from selling newspapers to collecting scrap to ashpit hunting. I collected cardboard and anything that was metal. Metals were really in demand then, because of the war. Usually if I got a dollar and a half for my collection of glass, cardboard, and metals, I was tickled to death. I used to haul it in a wagon to the junkyard. A favorite memory of mine during the war is that sometimes the Highway Theater, which was located only a block and a half away, would let you in free if you had aluminum or a stack of newspapers.

Wartime toys

Wartime freight trains made from heavy duty paper stock

Paper dolls

Puzzles

Games

Compasses

Anything with military insignias

No toys could be made that contained more than 7 percent, by weight, of iron, steel, zinc, or rayon.

Stuck in an Orphanage

Gerald Schriedel, born 1933

My mother had seven children in seven years. After she had the seventh, the doctor told the priest and my father we would all be orphans if she didn't have a complete hysterectomy. So she had one. Mother had a physical and nervous breakdown and didn't really recover. She was having a really tough time, looked like hell, and had a broken heart. On July 4, 1942, my parents dropped six of us kids off at the German St. Vincent Orphan Home in Normandy. I didn't want to let go of my dad's hand. We were all crying, all six of us. They dropped off the youngest in September, when he turned two. Mother had a red dress on, red lipstick. She looked at peace.

The Sisters of Charity took real good care of us. They were very caring and loving. I got thirty some letters from Dad, about forty letters from Mother. We had long school days. Every other Friday night, the boys went to the movie theater across the street. The girls went the other Friday night. We went on picnics and a couple overnights. We were bullied a lot in the beginning, because everybody else was an orphan. They asked, "What's it like to have a parent?" On December 18, 1945, my parents came to get us back and brought us on a train to their new home in Michigan. I remember that night we got in the house, when finally everything felt like being at home.

Turning to Delinquency

With dads off to war and moms working at defense plants, some authorities worried that kids left alone might turn into juvenile delinquents. In St. Louis, a commission formed by the mayor suggested a curfew for teenagers as a way to keep them off the streets. The St. Louis Board of Education created Wartime Child Care Centers to take care of the children of women who worked in essential industries. "Here is a problem that is approaching a national scandal," declared FBI director J. Edgar Hoover.

The News of Pearl Harbor

Betty (Cole) Falkenberg, born 1936

I know we were listening to the radio. It seems to me it was late in the day because we had washed our hair and we were sitting in front of the register to dry it. I was little, only five years old. I remember sitting, listening to Roosevelt tell us about Pearl Harbor.

The Mayor of Kinloch

Claretta K. Head, born 1939

The only two white people in Kinloch were a priest and this man named Mr. Raymond who was married to this black lady named Miss Carrie. My Uncle Willie Head was the first black mayor in the state of Missouri. He incorporated Kinloch.

We had everything in Kinloch. We had grocery stores, liquor stores, a restaurant, a movie theater, and a doctor. We even had a bank out there at one time. It was so quiet when you first got in town. That was what we called "the bottom." Then when you got up farther, that was "the hill," and it seemed like for some reason, the hill people and the bottom people were always getting into altercations, actual fist fights with one another.

What I can remember about World War II was there was a shortage of things like sugar and stockings. And I remember they used to have to have the shades down at night so nobody would see if they were in the house.

An Explosion of Kids

The Baby Boom was the expected result of a generation holding off during the Depression and the war. The marriage rate in 1932 was a measly eight per thousand total population, the lowest since after the Civil War. The rate slowly crawled out of that pit and then zoomed after V-E Day to a high of more than sixteen marriages per thousand total population in 1946, more than twice the 1932 rate and highest since just after the Civil War. The babies quickly followed.

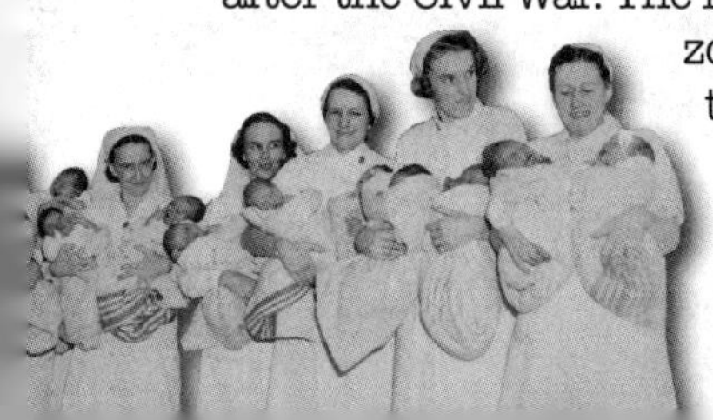

Alone on a Train

David Stevens, born 1940

I lived two years in the country when I was five and six, and that's where I went to first grade. My mom was ill and had some people down there who would take care of me. I took a train to Golden City with a note on my coat, all by myself at just five years old. I remember the porter smacking my hand because I picked up the silverware in the dining car.

I came back when I was in second grade. My father wasn't around anymore, and my mother was a keyboard operator downtown at Stix Baer & Fuller. Twice a month, something like that, I took a bus downtown to meet her after work. Her payday was on Thursday, and we'd go to a restaurant and a movie. We'd go see a movie I loved, like *Bambi*, at one of the theaters downtown like The Ambassador or Loew's State, I can't remember them all now. The theater buildings were just awesome. There were actually sculptures in mezzanines and carpeted floors.

Ambassador Theater interior.

A Welcome Home

Helen (Emery) Hannibal, born 1940

It was Christmas Eve, 1945, and we lived in a four-family flat on Ethel Avenue in Richmond Heights. My dad didn't put up the tree until about an hour before everybody was home. My dad was really good with the Christmas tree, taking care of it, making sure it was watered, because they were all real back then, not artificial.

The husband of the lady right across the hall was away in the war, but word came that he was going to be coming home. She had kept her Christmas tree up so they could have Christmas when he came home, even though it had to be January by then. Anyway, she kept that tree going. She said if my father would keep our tree then she could too, and her husband could have a nice Christmas. They didn't know exactly what day it would be until he came, and they waited so long that eventually all the needles fell off, and her Christmas tree was ruined.

About a week after Christmas, the woman found out her husband would be coming home. So she knocked on our door, and she said, "Bring your tree over, he's coming home!" So my dad took our tree. He left the ornaments on it, the tinsel, the star, and everything, and carried it sideways out of our apartment, and into the woman's apartment. There, he put it into the front window. I guess the woman's husband came home, came to Richmond Heights on the bus. He walked down the street and into the house, and there she was in the hall, with a Christmas tree waiting for him.

No More Fear of Snakes

Ellis Brown II, born 1942

At a very young age, we used to go to the zoo regularly. One of the highlights of it was when they got Miss Jim the Elephant. Me and my brother got to ride Miss Jim, a giant elephant. When you're four or five years old, all elephants are giants.

I always insisted on going to the Snake House. Mom would say, "No, because you'll have nightmares when we go home." Next time we'd go to the zoo, I'd say, "I want to go to the Snake House." She'd say "No, you're going to have nightmares." Then I'd insist, "I'm older now. I can do it." Each time, I'd explain to her, "I'm older, Mom, I won't have nightmares anymore." But, of course, I did. This went on until I was ten. And it's a good thing I finally got over that fear. You know why? I caught my first snake when I was in Boy Scouts the very next year, when I was eleven.

No Men Around

Paul Hartke, born 1943

I remember that there were no adult men around. Everybody was gone. My dad was gone before I was born. He was in the Army. The only adult male of that generation that I remember was my uncle, who didn't get drafted because he was six foot seven. I was almost three before my dad got back. He had been carrying a photograph of an infant, and he came home to a kid who was practically reading the newspaper.

I was always precocious, picking up on things I shouldn't have, and I suppose that's where I first heard that terrible word. It was a word that I wasn't supposed to know. After all, I was less than five. I don't know where I first heard it, but at some point I said it in front of Mom. She didn't like it one bit and decided that she was going to teach me a lesson. The next trash day, I was taken by the hand out to the alley to meet the trash man. And at that time, all of the trash men were black. That was what the word was about. We had a long conversation about him, his family, his children. He was a normal person, like everybody else. And he didn't deserve to be called that name, she made sure I understood that right then and there.

The whole family taught me through their actions, too. Like keeping our house clean inside and outside. The people who kept their houses that clean were called the South Side Scrubby Dutch. My grandmother on my dad's side was one of them. It was a ritual. All the housewives on the block started on the back of the house and worked their way to the front. The front door would come open, and they would back out of the house with the mops and the buckets, scrubbing away. By 10:30 in the morning, they were out there. Depending on what day of the week it was, they'd go on to somebody's house for coffee afterwards. It was almost choreographed.

OPEN 24 HOURS

Beaver's Decade
1950–1959

Family, the kind everyone saw in the sitcom *Leave It To Beaver*, ruled in the 1950s. So did turmoil, in the increasing tension of the Cold War and the Civil Rights movement. Those who came of age during the Depression and World War II poured their lives out on their kids. Kids dominated the drive-ins, the movies, and the new medium of TV. They were everywhere in the new subdivisions. But the Baby Boomers' first years were far from the tidy life of *Leave It To Beaver*, in which every problem resolved itself in a half hour. Kids were free from fear when they roamed neighborhoods. But they also had to hide under their desks to protect themselves from the bomb. Just about all of them figured out it was a useless exercise. That fear dominated much of the decade. The Supreme Court's order to integrate the schools brought kids into the civil rights battles. It added up to a moment of uneasy peace for children and the promise that life would be more complicated in the decades to come.

Locally, the St. Louis Public Schools switched to integrated classes the year after *Brown v. Board of Education*—Supreme Court decision that outlawed school segregation. But many whites fled to the suburbs. That, and the desire to go someplace new, caused Ferguson's population to double during that period. The population of Florissant multiplied tenfold in that time, while Bridgeton's population skyrocketed from 202 in 1950 to 7,820.

While whites settled into their newfound suburban homes, people of color stayed behind. In St. Louis, many lived in Pruitt Igoe, a high-rise apartment complex that replaced the slums northwest of downtown. Crews demolished the complex in the 1970s. Experts also thought the demolition of fifty-six hundred severely dilapidated homes in the Mill Creek Valley west of downtown was best, but in doing so they destroyed a black community of about twenty thousand. Racism made life harder, but some things are universal, regardless of race. Eric Jenkins, who lived in a four-room house in a predominantly black neighborhood in the

Brentwood-Richmond Heights-Clayton area, started each Saturday like most kids, watching TV and then going outside to play cowboys and Indians and other games until lunch. He did chores and jumped on his bike and rode around the neighborhood. "My only order was to come home before the streetlights came on," he said.

Everyone—regardless of race—was scared of polio. At its worst, pools closed and movie theaters urged patrons to sit apart from each other. The malady infected more than four-hundred thousand in the country from 1937 to 1955, by the time the first people received the Salk polio vaccine that halted the epidemic. No hope existed for those already paralyzed, but people tried to give them hope. In the summer of 1952, the Anheuser-Busch Clydesdales clomped by St. Anthony's Hospital at Grand Boulevard and Chippewa Street to bring cheer to polio patients.

Even more serious than polio was the possibility of an atomic attack. After the Soviet Union set off its first atomic explosion, the Federal Civil Defense Administration encouraged schools in some cities to teach children how to duck under desks and cover their heads when they saw a nuclear flash. It commissioned a New York company named Archer Films to produce a film about a smiling turtle named Bert who retreated inside his shell whenever an atomic blast went off.

Then there were fears brought on by one horrific incident on September 28, 1953: the kidnapping of six-year-old Bobby Greenlease from a Catholic School in Kansas City. Bonnie Heady picked him up at the school, claiming to be an aunt fetching her nephew after his mother had a heart attack. Her accomplice, Carl Austin Hall, shot the boy through the head and buried him in a shallow grave. The kidnappers collected a $600,000 ransom and headed to St. Louis, where their wild drinking and spending attracted the attention of the police. They died together in the gas chamber. In the aftermath, parents were more careful about letting their kids wander freely.

The incident made parents more cautious, but they still allowed their children a certain freedom, with toys to make their time outside more fun. At Christmas, parents gave toys or music. They often went to new shopping centers like Crestwood Plaza and brought their kids along. Eating habits changed after the first McDonald's in Missouri opened in 1958 at 9915 Watson Road in Crestwood. Kids could go anywhere, in fact, as long as they were home by supper time. After shopping trips or eating at McDonald's, parents chauffeured their youngsters to entertainment centers like the Esquire, Forest Park Highlands, or the zoo.

The zoo's chimpanzee and lion shows entertained kids. So did the seals, snakes, and tigers. For many, the complete visit to the zoo included a stop to see Phil the Gorilla. Phil charmed St. Louis with his playfulness.

Everybody loved Phil, but they loved Stan Musial even more. Musial was a superstar in a decade when the Cardinals marked time between pennants. He and the rest of the Redbirds hung out in Busch Stadium, the name Gussie Busch gave to the former Sportsman's Park when he bought it for Anheuser-Busch. Team owner August Busch Jr. had planned to name it Budweiser Stadium, but league rules prohibited naming a venue after an alcoholic beverage. Busch named the stadium after himself and later created Busch Beer.

That's the way it was in the '50s. Grownups may have done plenty of scary things, but for the most part, the decade was a time for kids to play outside with their friends, oblivious to the world around them. Their parents fashioned their world from the hope that their kids would have things better than they did. That would become more difficult in the next decade.

Best in His Class

Robert (Bob) C. Mueller, born 1936, retired manufacturing company owner

When all the rest of my shop class was making shoe boxes, I was making three-tier tables and end tables. I built all the furniture in our house, and by my second year in high school, I built a full-size rowboat. I felt like I was wasting my time, so I dropped out of Hadley Technical High School in the middle of tenth grade.

I found a company in Cape Girardeau that made waffle irons. They were paying thirty-five people to polish the outside of the irons before they plated them. Plating's what you do to add the mirror-like shine. I built a machine that did all that in six operations with one worker. It was a lot cheaper than those thirty-five workers and did a better job. So they let the workers go. That was just one of the projects I did after I dropped out of high school. When all my buddies graduated from high school, I was already showing a profit of five thousand dollars a week.

Eradicating Polio

More than 15,000 people in the United States were paralyzed each year by polio in the early 1950s, prior to the introduction of the first vaccine in 1955. The annual number fell to less than a hundred in the 1960s and less than ten in the 1970s. The last case from the United States was in 1979.

The Pains of Integration

Florida Cargill, born 1939

Florida Cargill

I attended the all-black school here in Webster Groves, Douglass High School on Holland Avenue, from kindergarten to eleventh grade. In September 1956 our high school was integrated into Webster Groves High School. At that time I was in the twelfth grade, Douglass High School was the only accredited high school in St. Louis County and Jefferson County that black children were able to attend. If the school you attended wasn't accredited, you couldn't go to certain colleges. June 1956 was the last graduating class of Douglass High School, and June 1957 was the first integrated graduating class of Webster Groves High School. Out of the 350 graduating students, there were fourteen African American students.

Our African American teachers were very serious about us attending Webster Groves High School and making a good impression. They made sure that we were well ready to integrate into the Webster High atmosphere, and Webster High didn't want the same thing to happen in Webster Groves that was happening at Little Rock High School and all the other places with the segregationist protests. So we had practice sessions at Douglass High, and we had to have white partners upon our arrival. If you got up there, every senior had to have a white partner during classes, to walk in the halls, etc.

Nevertheless, it was a lot of getting used to. There were certain things that they didn't allow us to know that the white kids were involved in that we weren't welcome to join at that particular time. For example, if you had dark skin, you could not be in the choir according to the choir director. If you weren't really light, like almost white, you would not be in her choir. Even though there were so many of us that had come from Douglass High that were really good in the choir and wanted to sing, she did not allow them to sing.

Out Until the Streetlights Came On

Cora (French) Katzen, born 1943

I grew up in the most wonderful neighborhood of all, South St. Louis, one and a half blocks from Shaw's Garden and three blocks from Tower Grove Park. Those were my playgrounds. The center street, Shenandoah, was tree lined, forming an arch over the street. We walked to school, we walked to the Admiral, we walked to shop, we knew almost all of our neighbors, and they knew us. Back then there were no bomb threats, no terrorists, no guns, no gangs. There were movie theaters we could walk to, doctors, dentists, clothing stores, shoe stores, candy stores, and even a smelly place where you could choose a live chicken to be butchered for Sunday dinners! We played outside until the streetlights came on and were free to just be kids. That meant we could play hide and go seek, kick the tin can in the alleys, hide out in the ash pits, climb trees, and roam in the parks.

When Ringling Brothers came to town, I went downtown, by myself, to join the circus. Another time, I saddled a horse and rode it over to Forest Park; I didn't think of it as stealing because I had seen other people do it. Of course, the horse threw me off. I walked back home with skinned knees and blood running down my legs.

Cora (French) Katzen (center)

Newsboy

Michael Quinn, born 1944

My mom was a housewife and my dad worked with newspapers, driving a route for the *Post* and *Globe*. I started going out with him when I was eight years old. We delivered newspapers to the apartments in Canterbury Gardens on Saturday nights. We'd wait for the newspaper man who delivered about three, four, or five hundred newspapers that we'd have to stuff with all the ads. Then we had to deliver them. We'd put them on the floor by the door. By seven o'clock in the morning, we were through, just in time to go to Sunday Mass.

The nuns there were funny when they got mad, and I pushed their buttons on more than one occasion. I had a nun grab me by the hair and give me a slap on the face. "Does that hurt?" she asked me. When I said "No," she was as mad as hell.

Remembering Christmas

Holly Farmer, born 1945

My parents had a house in Rock Hill that had really tall ceilings, and my mother would put up the Christmas tree every year by herself, and she'd have to get up on a ladder. We went downtown to Famous Barr to meet Santa Claus. On Christmas morning, we got up and looked to see if Santa Claus had come and then we opened our presents. At Christmastime, it was usually cold. I remember sliding down Art Hill in all the snow, and it was cold. We prayed that we didn't go into the lake at the bottom of the hill.

Toys

- Silly Putty
- Barbie doll
- BB gun
- Slinky
- Lincoln Logs
- Radio Flyer wagons

Communion, then Hot Chocolate and Glazed Donuts

Lois Tegethoff, born 1945

I went to a grade school that we could walk to, Our Lady of the Pillar, right next to Chaminade. There was a little gravel path you walked down between two homes. I used to wish there was a little train going down that path that sold candy. The path went down a hill, and then it came to a concrete bridge, and then there was a path that was paved from there to Chaminade High School. There was a little creek under the bridge where I learned how to ice skate.

We were Catholic, and I went to Mass twice a day in the morning. Early, early with my father and then with my regular school class. These were the days when if you fasted to go to Communion, you got hot chocolate and hot glazed doughnuts afterward. Everyone went to Communion. When I went to Mass with my father, that was just to go to Mass. When I went with my grade school, that was when you got the hot chocolate and the doughnuts—hot glazed doughnuts, just made. Fresh.

On Fridays in my family, my father brought home "payday." That was what we called the big bag of candy he brought for me and my two brothers. Penny candy, Mary Janes, those little bottles that had liquid in them. There was Baby Ruth. There were the little cigarette packages. Wax lips and wax teeth, you chewed them up. Maybe a little Life Savers, nibs licorice. The neighborhood kids would sit on the grass waiting for my dad to come. We'd all be out there waiting for him on Fridays. You'd see him coming, and he'd go down the driveway. "Mr. Tegethoff's here! Mr. Tegethoff's here!" He wouldn't give the candy to them, but they all knew he had it. I think we gave them some of our candy later. We'd share.

Growing Up Jewish in Kirkwood

Fred Blumenthal, born 1946

Fred Blumenthal

When I was ten months old, my father got a job at St. Louis University teaching pathology, and we moved to Kirkwood, not inside the Jewish neighborhood. They wanted to have more individuality, I guess, and mix in with real Americans. Though I'm not exactly sure why they decided to move there. We wound up in Kirkwood, and that's where my older brother and I went to public schools, kindergarten through high school. I think any sense that we were different was mostly in my own mind. I don't know that I was treated differently. I was aware that on Sunday mornings, they went to church, and we had other traditions.

Once I had done something naughty, though now I don't remember exactly what it was. The teacher's question to me was, "Was that the Christian thing to do?" I suspect even then, I really understood what she was asking, was it the fair-minded thing to do? Was it charitable? Was I being nice to this other child? But instead I answered, "Well, I'm not Christian." If I could go back and relive that moment, I think I would have fessed up a little more, and given the teacher a little less lip.

My parents brought us up in, let's say, a liberal way. We didn't keep kosher or observe all the various Jewish traditions. We did have Christmas trees. All of the neighbors had Christmas trees, so we had a Christmas tree, too. Except if my father's parents came to visit during that time of year. Then we wouldn't have a Christmas tree, because we couldn't confront them and disappoint them that we were following a Christian custom.

Delivering Moonshine

Darrell L. Fuse, born 1947

My name's Darrell Fuse, and I am the other brother Darrell. My mother had a son that didn't make it. His name was with one "L." Mine's with two. I grew up on the Hill, Catholic, went to St. Ambrose, and went to Shaw School. My claim to fame is that my grandmother was arrested in 1938 for moonshining. I used to deliver booze for her. And my mom and dad got busted in '57 for taking payments for my grandmother. She was in the same prison in '38 where Martha Stewart was in 2004. We laugh about it all the time.

I kept the tradition of working in the family like my mom and dad. First, I was shanghaied into the restaurant business when I was nine years old, sweeping floors for my Uncle Roy Russo's restaurant, called Rossino's. Then when I was twelve years old, I was making pizzas for my Uncle Charlie Gitto.

Darrell and Dorina Fuse talk with Santa.

Easing the Grief

Shirley (Kubina) Gebhardt, born 1947

I lived with my mom, dad, and big sister in a small brick house near Gravois and Loughborough. One night when I was ten, my Mom left home to play Bingo. Around 10:30 p.m., some friends brought her home quite sick. She passed out in a bedroom, and my dad called for an ambulance. A neighbor stayed with us while Dad followed the ambulance. He came home later with the saddest look and told us Mom had died of a massive heart attack on the way to the hospital. He said he lost the love of his life.

After that, he sometimes took us kids out for dinner just to do something different. We'd sit outside and listen to Harry Caray broadcasting ballgames. We'd go to the Granada movie theater near the Bevo Mill. I got him interested in bowling at the Red Bird Lanes. When we got too sad, we'd go see his friends Steve Mizerany and Joe Farhatt at the Mizerany store on Broadway. They cheered him up.

School Picnic

Mary (Kubiak) Schroeder, born 1948

The school picnics for Our Lady of Fatima School were always at Chain of Rocks Park, an amusement park built in the late twenties. Those picnics were wonderful, even if they were always the same. We'd always go there in the morning, and the mothers would all congregate under the huge pavilion. At least it seemed huge. A lot of the North County schools used that as their place for school picnics. This was the time when the mothers could say to their children, "Just come back at noon, and you go and ride the rides." They'd usually give you a string of tickets. Then you could choose which rides you wanted to use the tickets for.

1950s McDonald's Menu

Hamburger: 15 cents

Cheeseburger: 19 cents

Shake: 20 cents

Golden French Fries: 10 cents

Coke, coffee, soda: 10 cents

Called Home by a Cowbell

John Burns, born 1948

John Burns stands guard.

I moved to Ferguson in 1951. My mother's cowbell was the precursor to the smartphone. We had kind of a herd mentality. There were twenty kids living on the same cul-de-sac with us. We got kicked out of the house in the morning during summer and had to come back for dinner. The cowbell was how she communicated with us. We ran around and did all kinds of things until that cowbell rang.

We were all on the same party line, and you knew when someone got on the phone, if you were talking, you got off. "Oh, it's you." "OK, I'll call them back later." Then finally, the phone man came in to separate phones to give everyone a private line. So the phone guy going to each of the houses came to my home, and he says, "Are you all related?" and my mother says, "No, why do you say that?" "Well, all the kids ran to this house, and then they went through all of the houses."

Where I lived in Ferguson, the Wabash train that went downtown would sound a horn in the evenings. To me, it was like a familiar friend. At night, when you heard that, it was kind of saying everything's OK. It's always stuck with me. And later on, when I visited my grandmother in Pittsburgh, they had a streetcar that made the same noise as it went down the rails. I loved that familiar sound.

A Terrible Disease

Margaret (Tinius) Walker, born 1949

I got very sick with polio when I was three. I was burning up with an extremely high fever, and I was so sick, and in severe pain. I just remember waking up in the middle of the night and walking to the doorway of my mother's bedroom. I cried out, "Mom, Mom," and then I blacked out and fell because I couldn't stand anymore. The next thing I remember is hearing my mom and dad panicking. They grabbed me and put me into a blanket, and lay me on the floorboard of the car, all the while panicking and getting upset.

We went to Children's Hospital, and they refused me. They said they were full. Then they took me to St. Anthony's Hospital, and they accepted me. Everybody was terrified they would get polio back then, because they thought it was contagious. I woke up in an iron lung, and I was terrified. If I looked up with my eyes, I would see a mirror. I couldn't turn my head or anything, but I couldn't turn anyway. I was like a rag doll, so weak that I couldn't move anything. And there were things hooked up to me. All I remember is a bunch of tubing, maybe four in each of my legs.

It was a horrible experience. They wouldn't let anybody in to visit, and you couldn't even have a toy. You had nothing. You just lay there for the machine to breathe for you. They would send in one nurse to check on you. Once in a while, I think I saw a couple of men who were probably doctors. My dad pretended he was a minister, and he came in with a Bible and a little dolly for me. I saw the dolly next to me, and the nurse grabbed it, and she said, "I'm gonna burn this." They were so terrified of polio, that I guess they really didn't know what to do with it.

I almost died from the disease, and I stayed in total isolation for nine and a half months. It took years of rehabilitation and physical therapy just so I could sit up, feed myself, and eventually stand using long leg braces and arm crutches. Still, it left me with wasted away muscles, cells, nerves, and much deformity.

Christmas at Edgewood

Michael Hennon, born 1949

I lived at the corner of Gore and Rock Hill at Edgewood Children's Home. However, I did not live in one of the cottages. I lived in the director's house on the corner. During much of my time there, we had this big dirt hill outside of our house between the cottages and where I lived. Sometimes, I would go over and play with the kids at the residential treatment center. I remember walking to my first grade school, which was in Bristol. There was a little girl in my class who was a resident of the children's home. My father told me, "Don't tell them that you know her from here," because they still had concerns about protecting the privacy of those children.

Michael Hennon with her sisters Kathleen (left) *and Pat in front of the fence to their backyard at the corner of Gore Avenue and Rock Hill Road in Webster Groves.*

Christmases at Edgewood were sad, but it was a little bit more fun to celebrate the Fourth of July. My family would join the kids in the children's home, and down to the Shriners Day Circus, and we would go to the Highlands. Eventually the Highlands burned down. I remember seeing the smoke from the fire while I was walking home to Brentwood from my job as a caddy at Algonquin Country Club.

Hiding from the Bomb

Harriet Backhaus, born 1949

I was seven when Sputnik was launched. I was in the first grade. They would show us these filmstrips and films about this nuclear attack, and we would practice hiding under our desks. We got down on the floor, against a wall, or got under our desk. It was extremely frightening for a first grader. We saw these cartoons of Bert the Turtle. First, they would have a little song, and they would sing “Duck and Cover.” And then they would show Bert the Turtle ducking his head inside his shell. I was scared to death. The images still remain in my mind. I would be out on the play yard thinking that at any minute, the sky would light up, and we would be consumed by this nuclear weapon. They showed the films of the trees going this way, the paint being blown off the house, and I remember being really terrified, like I didn’t want to sit next to a window. The films showed the trees blowing one way then snapping back and blowing the other way as the blast came and went, like trees in a hurricane. It really bothered me for a long time.

Bert the Turtle

Stay Away from Phil

Jack Cowan, born 1949

My mother took me to the zoo when I was probably about six or seven years old. While we were there, she took me by the cage of Phil, the famous gorilla. There was a whole bunch of people standing in front of Phil's cage. Phil was lying there, and all of a sudden he got up and walked over to his pool, reached down and threw this wave of water at people who ran out of the way. And then Phil ran back and turned his back on everyone. After a while, everybody walked up to the railing again, and Phil turned around, reached out, and sent another wave of water out at people, forcing them to run to get out of the way. Phil turned around again, and the crowd walked back up to the railing. That gorilla splashed the crowd one more time! And I watched all of this. Standing back away from the water, I turned to my mother and said, "Mother, why do people keep going up there when they know he's going to splash them with water?"

Phil

1950s Elvis Movies

Love Me Tender (1956)

Loving You (1957)

Jailhouse Rock (1957)

King Creole (1958)

Close to a Master

James Horne, born 1951

My dad had a refrigeration repair business. He fixed big commercial units for stores, bars, florists, any place that couldn't afford to see them break down. I often tagged along on appointments. One hot summer day when I was about six, I found myself in a bar on the Hill while my dad repaired a beer-refrigeration system. "Hey, kid, you want to meet Yogi Berra?" someone asked me. I thought he said, "Yogi Bear," the bear from the TV cartoon show. Then from a stool next to me, a man said, "Sorry, kid, I'm not Yogi Bear. I'm Yogi Berra."

Yogi Berra

Yogi Bear

Learning Baseball from a Pro

Monroe Smith Jr., born 1952

My dad barnstormed in the Negro Leagues down in Mississippi with the Memphis Red Sox. The story that's better for me is how he turned me into a baseball player. He played semipro baseball in Tandy Park in front of Sumner High School in the 1950s. But the year he broke his ankle sliding into home plate was the year that my Little League baseball career started. That's when he started coaching us. The first year, he got sixty boys and eight dads on a baseball diamond in Fairground Park. Out of those sixty boys, three teams came about. We were some of the first teams in Mathews-Dickey Boys & Girls Club. Dad would get all kinds of things for the team. He got his company to sponsor our uniforms. Our block units sponsored our uniforms and equipment as did some of his friends who owned businesses.

We went to a barber shop, and back in those times, the African American players in the Cardinals and visiting teams could not stay at the hotels, so any time a black player came in from out of town, they stayed in a rooming house near the barber shop. It was my neighbor's shop. We got to meet everyone, Willie Mays, Hank Aaron, and Jackie Robinson, all of the famous African American baseball players of that time. We also got to meet football and basketball players all at this one barber shop, because it was walking distance from the boarding house. Curt Flood came to the shop to get his hair cut and to socialize. Because he was shorter and smaller than my dad, I said, "Dad, who is that guy?"

Willie Mays

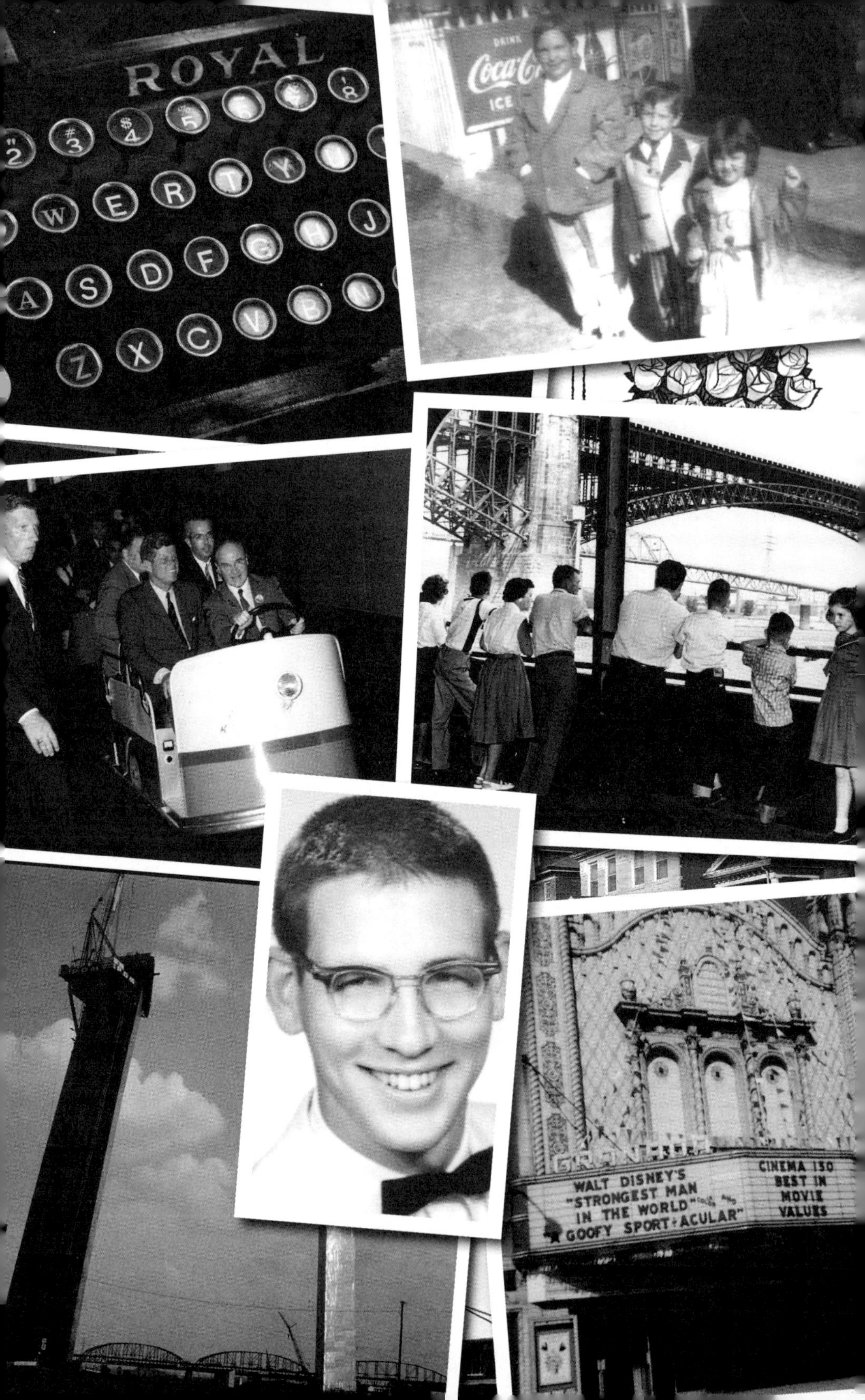
ROYAL
DRINK
Coca-Cola
ICE
WALT DISNEY'S
"STRONGEST MAN
IN THE WORLD" COLOR AND
GOOFY SPORT-ACULAR"
CINEMA 150
BEST IN
MOVIE
VALUES

Hope Dashed
1960–1969

Americans began the 1960s in what may have been the most optimistic moment of the Twentieth Century. A handsome young president declared that Americans would go to the moon by the end of the decade. Racial injustices that hung over from the Civil War seemed ready to end. But the mood turned ugly with assassinations, the war in Vietnam, and more racial turmoil.

In St. Louis, construction of the Gateway Arch caught everybody's imagination, while builders of new highways blasted their way out of the city and into the far reaches of the area. They split neighborhoods and made it easier for white St. Louisans to escape the city. Kids who once played on crowded city streets rode their bikes on spacious suburban streets. To keep up with all the new students moving to formerly-rural areas, districts like Lindbergh and Parkway busied themselves erecting new schools.

When students from those schools got home, they often watched kiddie shows. Many St. Louis kids watched those shows but preferred sports. The decade brought the end of the Stan Musial era and a move of the Cardinals from the ramshackle Sportsman's Park to the new Busch Memorial Stadium downtown. The Cardinals overcame the Yankees in the 1964 World Series, beat the Red Sox in the 1967 Series, and lost the 1968 Series to the Tigers. Added to that mix were the football Cardinals, the basketball Hawks (until they moved to Atlanta in 1968), and the launch of the hockey Blues in 1967.

A sad moment came on November 22, 1963, when President John F. Kennedy was shot in Dallas. Most Americans over sixty-five still remember where they were when they heard the news. Generally, they heard about it in class, because it happened at midday. Everything was on hold until the Beatles flew in from Liverpool in February 1964 and jolted the kids and grown-ups back to life on *Ed Sullivan*. Things went back to normal, sort of, but nothing was the same after that. But, they still loved the music.

When they went to dances, they loved a local band leader named Bob Kuban. When the Beatles held a concert at the new Busch Stadium on August 21, 1966, people didn't love them so much. It was not long after that John Lennon made his ill-fated remark that the Beatles were "more popular than Jesus." Crowds were turned off, and the group played in a downpour, in a venue that was only half full. Things went so badly that Paul McCartney agreed with the other Beatles that it was time to stop going on the road. They finished their tour and never gave another concert.

When they weren't watching and listening to music, kids followed the construction of the Gateway Arch. The monument's height, 630 feet tall, happened to be the frequency of the rock-and-roll AM station KXOK. The station milked the coincidence in promotions that helped make it the station teenagers of the 1960s turned on as they did their homework. Many regretted the time a CBS crew spent at Webster Groves High School working on a documentary called *16 in Webster Groves*. They said it gave a misleading portrait of the school and the division between popular and unpopular sixteen-year-olds. One class member, Joseph Sohm, said interviewers asked approximately twenty students what they would do in their car, for example. Virtually all would give a wholesome answer. But there would be someone who would say something racy and was typically the answer the documentary would use. Now a nationally known photographer, historian, and public speaker, Sohm wasn't happy with the documentary. He figures he was in the program for about seven seconds—and that was seven seconds too long. But others said CBS got it right.

Some found it harder to understand the decade's civil rights protests. In 1963, Jefferson Bank & Trust Co. agreed to hire black tellers after months of protests. Other businesses followed, while protests for decent housing and jobs continued, along with nonviolent civil disobedience. The sometimes-violent protests led to civil rights legislation that offered the hope of a better life.

African Americans whose parents worked as laborers went to college and found work as schoolteachers or lawyers. St. Louis's William Lacy Clay Sr. found a job in Washington when he was elected Missouri's first African American congressman in 1968. After the passage of legislation prohibiting housing discrimination, many moved to the county. Ironically, that decimated African American enclaves like The Ville, driving away a customer base and causing African American-owned businesses to dwindle.

Many were united in the fight against what they saw as a pointless war in Vietnam. For some younger siblings of those who went to Vietnam, their war experiences didn't end when their big brothers returned. Almost all communities lost some of their precious young who had just become adults. Many had younger sisters and brothers still growing up. They still bear the wounds of losing a big brother far away. One local woman who worried about her big brother in Vietnam was Dolores Kemp, now Dolores Picker. She waited for the return of her big brother Robert Kemp from Vietnam in the two years before she graduated from Brentwood High School in 1968. After arriving in Vietnam in 1966, he did classified decoding of enemy communications for the Air Force. Dolores knew it wasn't as dangerous as some duty, but it still made her uneasy. Her family kept a map of Vietnam in the kitchen to watch the progress of the war. She considered protesters unpatriotic. After her brother came home, he said, "War is stupid." It was one of many signs of a hopeful time gone bad.

Waiting for JFK

Gregg McGee, born 1947

I was waiting on Madison Avenue, around where the Burger King is now, for the cars to come when John F. Kennedy came to Granite City during his 1960 campaign for president. The motorcade passed and Kennedy was sitting up on a seat in his convertible, on the very end. We got a good look at him and one of my first impressions was that he had a lot of hair. And that was it, really. Because Kennedy was Catholic, of course the Catholic schools got out to see him. All school kids from Sacred Heart Catholic School were there, young people. It was quite an event, of course. I'll remember that the rest of my life.

I was pretty impressed. My parents were Republicans, and they were going to vote for Nixon. But I had a sign on my door that I was voting for Kennedy. Of course, I couldn't vote at that time because I was too young. But I wanted him to win the election, which he eventually did.

A Born Reporter

Sterling Levy, born 1948, journalist

I did start doing things like writing fake news on that old Royal typewriter. Of course, I didn't look at it that way. I would pretend to be a sports writer and write reports of basketball games. Nothing that anybody saw. Maybe once in a while my cousin would see a copy of it. It was just fun to pretend that I was sitting there. I would write letters to family relatives out of town. I was pretty good at that. I worked for the high school paper, too. Of course, I found out it was pretty much who you know, and not what you know. It was destiny.

Double duty

It often fell to local TV weathermen in the 1960s to do a show for youngsters as well. Jim Bolen did his weather guy thing and played the star on *Cookie and the Captain* on KMOX-TV (Now KMOV). Clif St. James portrayed *Corky the Clown* on KSD (now KSDK). Harry Fender showed kiddie shorts on *Captain 11's Showboat*, but didn't have to do the weather. Other kid shows done by non-weatherfolk were *The Wrangler's Club* with Harry Gibbs, *Romper Room* with Miss Lois, and *Mr. Patches* with Jack Miller.

The Death of Kennedy

Joseph Winkler, born 1948

Joseph Winkler

I was fifteen years old. I was a sophomore at McBride, and we were in the world history class. It was just after lunch. The teacher was called out to the principal's office and when he came back, he told us all to be quiet. He said President Kennedy is dead, and we were of course just stunned. This was the kind of thing that happened to other people in our lives but not to us. We were all sent home, and I can remember riding a bus down Kingshighway Boulevard and looking out the window, and there were people on the street, but they weren't moving. They weren't going about their business. They were sort of standing. Some were crying. But most of what I remember is people standing there just stunned at what had happened. It was a long bus ride home. It was about an hour, and this is what I experienced the whole time. Nobody on the bus was talking. We were just, I don't know what you'd call it. I just think we were just floored by it.

Holy Water

Joseph Taylor, born 1949

I do remember once we took a field trip when I was in high school and saw the Arch during its construction. I remember seeing the Arch when the legs were high enough that they had to have the truss on them. We also went to the Old Cathedral and one of my friends, or maybe he wasn't a friend, went in and filled his squirt gun up with holy water.

A Costly Decision

William Quinlan, born 1950

When I was a senior at Southwest High School, I participated in helping put together an underground newspaper. There were kids from thirty-two or thirty-three high schools working together on it. The day it was published in 1969, while we were distributing issues, we were all kicked out of high school. I went to a form of night school for students who'd been expelled. There were kids that were kicked out for various reasons, including some girls who were pregnant. In those days, if you got pregnant, you finished in night school. It was just sort of a mixed group of kids. I don't remember if it was more than two or three months. I had always worked part time, and so I probably just continued to work part time. I had a fun job delivering groceries in the Central West End, and I traveled all over the city of St. Louis. From there, I went to Forest Park Community College.

Southwest High School

Very Personal Service

David Brendel, born 1953

My grandfather, my dad, and my aunt and uncle had grocery stores in South City. My dad and mom's store was at 6219 Arthur, where we lived above and behind the store. I worked after school and on the weekends with my older brother and younger sister who helped. We weren't allowed to be open on Sundays, though, because we went to church.

We had a lot of children in our neighborhood who came in while their parents shopped. I was in charge of a big candy case. We might charge ten cents worth of candy, which at that time was a lot of candy. It was all loose, so we'd give it to them in a little bag while their parents would buy bread and milk. We just added it to their bill, and they'd pay it at the end of the week. Besides the penny candy case, we stacked the groceries, canned goods, and toilet paper.

Left to right, in front of Brendel Market, John, David and Miriam Brendel.

We would deliver groceries to the houses at that time. Most of our customers were on the block, which meant we usually walked the delivery up or put it on our bikes. There were two more stores, one at the corner of our block, and one other at the other corner. Our customers lived pretty close at the time, and they relied on us because we carried everything in the store. We had fresh bread delivered, fresh bread and bakery goods every day. A lot of the railroad people used to come over and get their lunch. We were the neighborhood hangout, you might say, until we closed in 1966.

Double Dutch

Perkins Smith III, born 1955

We lived on the dividing line of the neighborhood within the neighborhood. Across the street from us was a lot of low-income apartments and slum lords. On our side were professionals and homeowners. There were three-story brick homes on our side of the street, which we would call mini mansions.

We knew how to entertain ourselves with normal stuff back then, like playing marbles. We didn't have all the electronic stuff. The whole neighborhood was family oriented, and we knew how to have a good time with each other. We didn't just jump rope, it had to be Double Dutch, using two ropes to make it harder, but more fun.

Perkins Smith III

The Ladue of the Ghetto

Gary Fort, born 1956, homeless

I grew up on a private, historic street, Lewis Place, over between Page and Delmar. This is where prominent African Americans lived, like doctors and teachers. Back during that time, it was considered the "Ladue of the Ghetto," like the fanciest suburb of St. Louis. Before my mother and father purchased the house we lived in, it was owned by an African American doctor. Her name was Dr. Ruth Harris. When I was little, I attended Washington School and on my way home, I used to stop at that house and play on the grass. I never knew that, one day, I would actually be living there. My mother and father bought the house and we stayed there for fifty years. The house was very nice. It had a driveway and a sun porch.

My father worked for the Board of Education. He was the head custodian of Mullanphy School off of Shaw. He ran the school, and I used to go with him while he put the coal in the furnace. My mother was a teacher, Ethel W. Fort. She was very strict with me. A lot of people didn't like me when I was growing up, because I was very fortunate. They used to call me a poor rich boy. I knew nothing about the projects. I didn't grow up on food stamps. When I was growing up, I thought I was rich. I had great Christmases, a dog, pets.

First Look at the Fab Four

Linda (Seiferth) Gurney, born 1956

I grew up in University City. I'm a professional musician and started learning music very, very early. I was already studying music for three years when I was seven years old, and we watched *Ed Sullivan* every Sunday like a lot of people. One night, it just happened to be the night the Beatles debuted on *Ed Sullivan*. I didn't know it was going to be anything particularly special, but, oh my gosh! The girls were screaming, and the Beatles had a sound I found very exciting, even in my young years, and I was transfixed by it. I remember going upstairs to bed. It was hard to wind down. I was laying on my back, and my legs were kicking. What a feeling. I never did forget that. And then, to cap that off, just days later, my father came home with the *Meet the Beatles!* album.

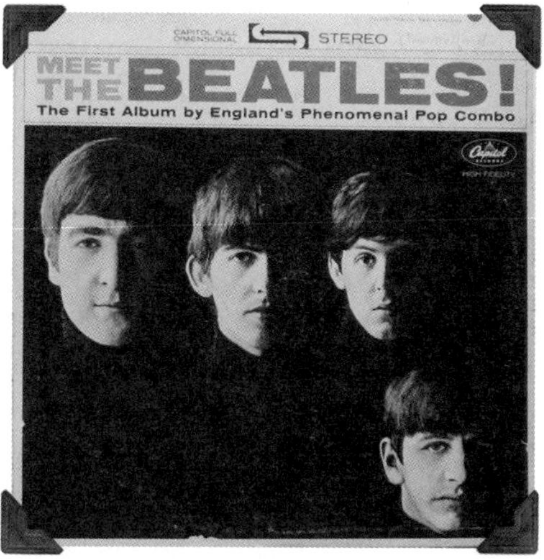

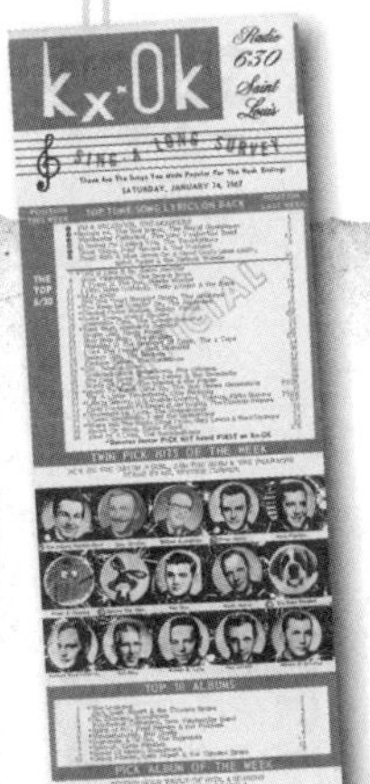

Top 40

Of all the teen radio stations since World War II, KXOK was the best in its heyday in the 1960s. Johnny Rabbitt, portrayed first by Ron Elz and then Don Pietromonaco, was a leading reason students didn't have their homework ready in time. Starting in 1967, the classical-semiclassical station KSHE-FM gave it serious competition when it switched to progressive rock.

Peace Through Greens

Anthony "Tony" Butler, born 1956

I didn't start encountering white folks in a social setting until we moved up to Walnut Park. It's experiencing an opposite culture, colors and stuff, one on one and everything. I had this friend after I moved out there. Their family had two sons, Frank and Mark. Frank was my age, and Mark was his little brother. Every blue moon, we'd invite Mark and Frank over for dinner. My mother would make greens, seasoned with ham hocks. Greens could almost be a meal in itself. The first time they experienced the greens, they couldn't stop talking about it. And they went home and told their mother about it to the point that one day their mother came over and said, "Where is your mother?" I went and got my mom, and she said, "Is there anything wrong?" And their mother said, "No, you've got to tell me how do you fix greens?" Because all her sons talked about was greens and the fried chicken. Oh, boy, my mother could fix fried chicken. But they turned me on to something, too. Lasagna.

Write Bob Burnes

Tom Wolf, born 1957

When I was nine, my dad took me to my first Cardinals baseball game. It was a Cardinals-Cubs game. It was bat night, and I was excited to get one. Back then, they gave you a full-sized bat. They didn't give you those little miniatures like they do now. It was a real bat. I want to say it was a Lou Brock, but I can't say for sure what it was. So of course, I took it home and went out and played baseball with it. And it broke.

I complained to my father the next day, "Dad, that bat broke." Dad sarcastically said, "Complain to the paper, write Bob Burnes." He was the predominant sports columnist at the *St. Louis Globe-Democrat.* I wrote a letter to Bob, and guess what he did? He published my letter in his columns. I couldn't believe it since I was just a little boy. He said those bats are really made for souvenirs, and that you shouldn't use them for play. It's not a bat that's competitive quality, but a kid wouldn't know that. I cut the article out of the newspaper and put it in my mother's scrapbook that she kept for me. Unfortunately there was a fire in my apartment after she had passed away and it was lost.

Two TVs Made Him Rich

Joe Holleman, born 1957, columnist, *St. Louis Post-Dispatch*

I was born in the Benton Park area and lived there until we eventually moved to the county. I was at Telegraph and 270 back when it was still considered country. We were the city kids who had moved to the county. So it was a suburban-type growing up, but there was a city feel to it in that every parent in my neighborhood was born and raised in the city before moving out there with their families.

Television was a big deal for us, and I was a *Corky* Kid. I remember *Captain 11*, too. A lot of it had to do with *The Three Stooges*. As a kid, that was the first show I remember. The teachers were worried we would come to school and poke each other in the eye. I started watching *Corky*. I remember getting a second television when I was little so my dad could watch his ball games in a back room on a small TV, and my mom could still watch her shows at the same time. I remember thinking we must be fairly rich because we had this second little black-and-white portable.

Holding Hands

Lolita (Jones) Paiewonsky, born 1958

As a recess playground assistant in the sixth or seventh grade at St. Joseph Parochial School in East St. Louis, Lolita (Jones) Paiewonsky thought she could take the hand of a second grader when necessary. But the little girl burst into tears and used a racial slur to say she couldn't touch a black person's hands.

The bottom line was, this is what the child had been taught at home. Of all the children in the school or even in that grade, I hadn't experienced anything like that.

Biting His Tongue

Jeff Lesher, born 1958

My family attended Tower Grove Baptist Church near Shaw's Garden. They have a roller skating rink in the basement of what they call the activities building, which is a really nice facility. They have a real nice gym, bowling alley, skating rink. Once, when I was probably less than five years old, I was sitting on a rail next to that skating rink. I wasn't even skating, because I don't even think I knew how to skate yet. But I jumped off, fell, and hit my chin on the floor. I had my tongue out, and I nearly bit my tongue off. They took me upstairs, put some ice in my mouth, but they ended up taking me to St. Anthony's Hospital at Chippewa and Grand, the same hospital I was born in.

I had actually bitten all the way through my tongue, The wound was connected on the sides. To put stitches in my tongue, they took a sheet and put my tongue through a hole in the sheet so I couldn't see what they were doing. Then they put it over my face and cut a slit in it. Next, they ran a piece of thread through the tip of my tongue which was deadened it so I didn't feel anything, and the nurse held that so the doctors could put the stitches in. After that, my tongue was swollen so much I could only eat milk shakes and stuff like that for a week and a half or two.

School Days

Antonina (Giardina) Heinzerling, born 1960

I went to grade school up at St. John the Baptist near the Bevo Mill in the city, and then my first two years of high school I went to St. John the Baptist High School, before eventually graduating from Cleveland.

The nuns? All the nuns I had, I had no problem with. They could teach thirty kids in a class with no problem. There was no such thing as ADHD. They just disciplined you, and you listened. It was a whole different atmosphere. None of them were mean to me. They were mean to kids that didn't listen. I developed the best penmanship from the nuns' discipline.

I do remember too the Granada Theatre, which was kind of in back of Bevo Mill restaurant. It's empty now. I would go with my brother to matinees like Disney and *Mary Poppins* on Sunday afternoons. It was fun. There was a banana ice cream stick that was really good.

Granada Theater

Falling in Love with Sports

Frank Cusumano, born 1961, Sports Director, KSDK TV

My dad was the best man I ever knew. He raised six rowdy kids and ran a restaurant called Kemoll's. He did it all with grace, dignity, and a real gentle quality. My mom, who is ninety years old, was an incredibly caring mother who wanted to be involved in every detail of my life. All eight of us worked at Kemoll's. I saw my dad being kind of a maître d'hôtel and greet every customer as kind of long lost friends. I was in the people industry at a young age.

Bob Gibson

My second oldest memory was him picking me up to go to the '68 World Series. We spent hundreds of baseball games together, and we never missed a St. Louis Cardinals football game. I saw Game One when Bob Gibson struck out seventeen for the record. My dad and I sensed that we were watching something that we would never forget. That moment was the moment that made me fall in love with sports.

Forest Park Highlands

For those who grew up in the 1950s and 1960s, something died when the Forest Park Highlands burned on July 19, 1963. Older Boomers may remember the amusement park on Oakland Avenue between Kingshighway Boulevard and Hampton Avenue for its school picnics, fun house, its swimming pool, and its roller coaster.

Playing in the Street

Colleen La Croix, born 1962

My parents had an apartment in the city by Christy Park. My dad thought it would be nice if we could move out to the county. He would go for drives around the county looking for houses. So finally, he found one in South County, where I spent the rest of my upbringing. We went back into the city to shop, because my mom was familiar with the city. Our house was a ranch-style home with a big yard in the Lindbergh School District. It was a really awesome, fun time because there were a lot of kids on our street—a cul-de-sac that ended at Bohrer County Park.

We could play on the entire street and go down to the park, where we could fish. My dad was a fisherman, so he had the supplies that we needed. If the pond froze, my mom would take us to skate. We learned to ice skate on that pond and we were outdoors a lot in the summertime. We were sometimes out until ten o'clock at night playing "sneak back to base," and flashlight tag and stuff like that, or looking up at the night sky. My dad was really into astronomy, and he'd tell us about the stars and the constellations.

Mister Softee

The ice cream trucks of Mr. Softee were Pied Pipers of the area's kids when they moved around our urban and suburban streets. The trucks lured the youngsters with Lester Waas's 1960 melody "Jingles and Chimes" on its loudspeaker.

326
POLICE

What's Going On?

1970–1979

After a decade of disappointment, the nation slogged through the 1970s in a funk. The outcome of the War in Vietnam marked the first time in history that the United States lost a war. While this was happening, the president was overseeing a dangerous criminal enterprise. Richard Nixon resigned as president, but the nation hobbled along for the rest of the decade through gas rationing and disco, until the decade ended with the humiliating seizure of the US Embassy in Iran.

In the St. Louis area, the county's population was slightly ahead of the city's in the 1960s census. But by 1970, the county had more than twice as many people as the city. For the largely white group of new suburban residents, the county and farther-out places like St. Charles and Jefferson counties were ideal places to raise kids. It wasn't as easy for those left behind in St. Louis.

The fight for educational equality was just part of the struggle of African Americans in the 1970s. They also fought against violence where they lived. Living in poverty in crime-filled neighborhoods, they found a simple exercise like walking outside was dangerous. Nonetheless, statistics showed African Americans were doing better economically. Civil rights legislation and strong government policies prohibiting discrimination for businesses with government contracts helped African Americans get better jobs and better wages.

Teenagers dealt with other trends, including a spike in the number of unmarried women having kids. Meanwhile, young people were among those caught up in a resurgence of religious activity. After the upheaval of the 1960s, many turned afresh to demonstrative forms of Christianity and brought their children with them. Songs like "Jesus is Just Alright With Me," and "Oh Happy Day" climbed the charts. The Charismatic Renewal, a repackaged form of Pentecostalism, brought speaking in tongues and prayers for healing to Catholics, Protestants, and those who previously had no religion. Locally, the Catholic Charismatic Renewal achieved cautious respect as adherents professed their beliefs at meetings at Visitation Academy, Our Lady of Perpetual Help parish, and elsewhere. Protestants expressed their newfound unity with Catholic brothers and sisters in this resurgence of faith.

Whatever their religion, kids loved to dance. When they turned on the radio, they heard stations like KADI and KSHE. Mark Klose, Joy Grdnic, and Ron Stevens spoke between the songs on KSHE. Clubs filled with kids dressed in polyester dancing to music from "Le Freak" and "Get Up and Boogie." High school students who could drive made it to concerts at Kiel Auditorium and Opera House, the Arena, or at the Mississippi River Festival at the Southern Illinois University at Edwardsville. Before it shut down in 1980, the festival drew crowds in the tens of thousands for nationally known bands and artists. Often, the smell of marijuana smoke lay thick in the air at such concerts. The songs varied, but Marvin Gaye's "What's Going On" was as good an anthem of the time as any.

Sports—from high school level to major league—also was a focus of kids and high school students in the 1970s. In their annual Turkey Day football game in the 1970s, the Webster Groves High School Statesmen won seven times, while the Kirkwood High School Pioneers won three times. Meanwhile, the baseball and football Cardinals racked up a so-so record but nonetheless were fun to watch. People knew Al "The Mad Hungarian" Hrabosky for his Fu Manchu mustache and his strange looking maneuvers meant to put batters off kilter. Even better for the youngsters, the Redbirds rolled out their secret weapon in 1979, their mascot, Fredbird. Games of the indoor soccer team the St. Louis Steamers included strobe lights and rock 'n' roll played in the Arena. "Bad News" Marvin Barnes became Rookie of the Year when he played basketball for the Spirits of St. Louis during the 1974-75 and 1975-76 seasons.

Teenagers may have loved their sports, but they filled the movie theaters to see classics like *American Graffiti*. The very young set their eyes on such cartoons and flicks as *The Muppets* or perennial favorite toys like GI Joes and Barbie dolls. For those whose idea of fun was much bigger than a toy, Six Flags Over Mid-America opened in Eureka on June 5, 1971.

The noise at Six Flags, the area's concert venues, and other places where kids played in the 1970s could have drowned out the sense of despond that many see in the decade. *St. Louis Post-Dispatch* reporter and columnist Joe Holleman, author of the book *Generation St. Louis: The Baby Boomer Years 1955-79*, offers that it wasn't a case of not noticing the despond of the time. "Trust me, the good brothers and teachers at Vianney would never have allowed that to happen," he said. Rather, it was more a case of "noticing the despondency, but also noticing that it wasn't part of our everyday lives." As they always did, the kids kept dancing, no matter how bad things got. When Marvin Gaye asked, "What's Going On?" most could only give Little Richard's answer, We're going to have some fun tonight!"

Pregnant at Fifteen

Jane (Dibble) Nelson, born 1956

I was raised in the Cherokee area. My mother worked all day. My father was a rolling stone. I found out later in life that I had ten siblings. I had always thought I was the youngest, but it turns out I'm the middle child.

I was pregnant at fifteen, got married at sixteen, and had my son in July of '73. I had a daughter and then I divorced. I remarried and had two more daughters. I persevered, worked my way up, and I'm a medical secretary now, and on my second marriage, going on thirty-sixty years now. My son unfortunately died in 1999, but I have my three daughters, and we've made it. Just getting pregnant at that early age, a lot of parents would have made me give him up for adoption, but that wasn't a choice for me, because I wasn't going to do it. I knew that my mother gave away a child when I was eleven months old. It was her choice, but I hated her for it. At the same time, I commended her for it, because she was able to provide another family with a child that they were not able to have. I found this brother in 2014. And I've also found all my other siblings from my daddy's side. We've got this big family; they're all down in Arkansas. That's why I've got this twang, I guess.

Grass and Concerts

Jeff Lesher, born 1958

I didn't go very often to high school. I was cutting classes at an astronomical rate, and I didn't do my homework, so I was failing everything. I got into rock 'n' roll music and smoking marijuana. I dropped out of school and went to work full time at my mother and father's flower shop. I went to a lot of rock concerts. The first concert I went to at the Arena was November 28, 1973, with The Who with Lynyrd Skynyrd opening for them. Another one was Led Zeppelin at the Arena in 1975. We camped for two days to get tickets in the second row. That was back when cigarettes or anything else you wanted to smoke you could smoke in the Arena. Plus you had fireworks. It was crazy the stuff that people got away with in concerts back then.

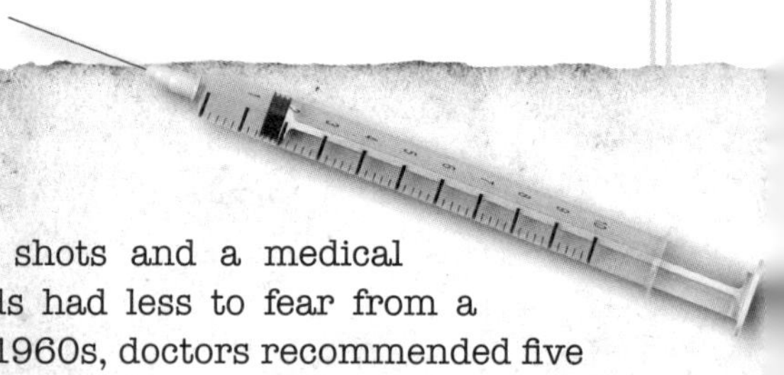

Fewer Shots

Combinations of vaccination shots and a medical success story meant that kids had less to fear from a visit to the doctor. In the late 1960s, doctors recommended five vaccines to be given in separate shots and three to be combined in one shot. After that, the number of separate shots was cut to three. The diphtheria, tetanus and pertussis vaccines were taken as one, as were the measles, mumps, and rubella vaccines. The polio vaccine was administered as one. Efforts to wipe out smallpox were so successful that the smallpox vaccine wasn't recommended after 1972. On the other hand, parents weren't treating their kids to ice cream as much after a visit to the doctor.

Memories of Mom

Dennis Kinealy, born 1958, homeless

My mom beat up the lady downstairs. She was a big gal, too, but my mom was just four foot nine. I don't remember why she beat her up, I don't know what the story was. I remember a kid in the third grade pushed me in the back of the head. I turned around, *POW!* It runs in the family, huh? He wouldn't knock it off.

My mom called me all kinds of names, like "stupid," "I wish you never were born." That kind of stuff. Right before she died, she said, "You're going to make me have a stroke. It'll be all your fault." I know what the real reason is. She had very high blood pressure, and she had stopped taking her blood pressure medicine. Instead, she went to some Kathryn Kuhlman spiritual healing service. That's what killed her. She thought she was healed. I remember before she died, her face was beet red. I just knew. It was July 27, 1975. She had a stroke in a church service before noon and died later in the evening at Missouri Baptist Hospital.

Movies teens loved

Jaws

Rocky

Saturday Night Fever

Star Wars

Something in the Water

Sharon (Schiller) Fusco, born 1962

I grew up in Florissant off Patterson Road. They had built a bridge off of Moule Drive over Coldwater Creek, and that's where I took the bridge to get to school every day. Everyone would end up going over the bridge to get to some land that wasn't developed. People would ride dirt bikes back there, or go play in the creek, where people would fish for crawdads. When it got super cold, I know my brother and his friends played hockey on the ice on the way to school in the morning. We were around Coldwater Creek all the time, because we lived three blocks, four maybe, from it.

At our high school reunion, we just felt it was odd, especially at our ten year reunion, to have already lost so many classmates. We had just graduated in '80; I didn't expect that many people to be deceased already. People were dying in their early twenties, and finally when there was a Facebook group called Coldwater Creek: Just the Facts, that stuff started coming out. There were so many odd cancers.

I still live here in Florissant. It was a wonderful place to live as a child, an idyllic place. I've raised both my kids here.

The cause of the cancers was radioactive waste from Mallinckrodt Chemical Works, which made fuel for the Manhattan Project atomic bombs in World War II at a plant downtown. Much of it was transported from Mallinckrodt in the city to near the airport. From there, the waste made its way into the environment, including Coldwater Creek.

Afraid at a Traffic Stop

John Hayden, born 1962, St. Louis Police Commissioner

My father was a big guy. I remember being pulled over by the police a few times, and I'd say, "Hey, Dad. What's going on?" He'd say, "Calm down, son." But each time, I'd look down and notice his hand shaking.

That was not like him to be uncomfortable. But, of course, he was born in 1928 and had lived in Louisville, Kentucky. He'd seen a lot of the Jim Crow discrimination kind of thing. He'd seen where police can do whatever they want to an African American and not suffer any consequences for it and so, I guess, even though it was in the 1970s, he felt nervous when we got pulled over. It really left an indelible impression upon me to see my big strong dad's hand shaking that way.

The Big Race

Melanie Young, born 1964

I grew up in University City in the ’70s. My neighborhood was pretty diverse at that time. We did have African American families and Caucasian families on our street. We had a couple of teachers that lived in the neighborhood who taught at my elementary school. It was a pretty close-knit neighborhood, as most neighborhoods were back in those times, where you knew your neighbors and they knew your mom and your dad or your family members.

One summer, all of the families on my block built go-karts. The kids did all the building, with the brothers and sisters as teams. We worked for a week or so getting different parts from old bikes and wagons and things using wood boards and stuff that we found in our garage. Then one evening we decided to race. We went to the very top of the block and were all teamed up with our siblings. Then we raced down the middle of the street. We all laughed and had a good time after talking about whose go cart was built the best. It was kind of like bragging rights. I don’t remember who won the race, but I think me and my brother were in second place or something.

We would play games in the evening with our friends in the neighborhood. We played hide-and-seek using the streetlight as the base. We would stay out during the summer months and do these types of things, or set out exploring and go through the neighborhood creek. My mom would have died if she knew we were in the creek, but in the end, nobody got hurt.

Toys

- GI Joe Astronaut
- Hot Wheels Track and Cars
- Barbie Dolls
- Bikes
- Simon Says

Wandering the Neighborhood

Ann Workman, born 1965

I grew up on the east side of Creve Coeur, so I went to Ladue High School. It was a wonderful neighborhood, the kind of place where my little brother and I could wander wherever we wanted. We had nice yards, so that was a good place to be. I actually live in my childhood home now. And my little brother, who's not so little anymore, lives with his family just two houses down the street from us. So his kids can walk back and forth to me, and I love that. It means they're going to have that same kind of childhood that my brother and I got to have.

Two Cents for a Tootsie Roll

James Patrick (Jim) Merkel (No relation to the author), born 1965

I remember walking to Heege School because it was right down the street. There was always a little convenience store right on the corner at Heege and Mackenzie. I know you could get a piece of gum for a penny or two. Or Tootsie Rolls. I remember buying the Tootsie Rolls because they were like maybe a couple pennies apiece. They were cheap.

The playground was good. It was big. We would have snack time out there and play on the swings, run around, and be maniacs. In the winter, I can remember making big old snowmen out in the big old field. I guess maybe those things just felt big to us. They were simple times.

Bands at local concert venues

Ella Fitzgerald

Janis Joplin

Chuck Berry

The Who

Lynyrd Skynyrd

Brothers Forever

Scott Epstein, born 1967

I have one brother, Mark, who was born quadriplegic in 1961. He was paralyzed from the shoulder blades down, but I didn't know anything else, he was just my brother. We got along real good, no problems. I mean, we had our fights, but it was probably just your typical brother-brother relationship. We loved going to amusement parks as a family. When we'd go to Six Flags, we could stay with him and go on the rides without waiting in the lines. He went on the Screamin' Eagle and the Mine Train. My dad would carry him on the ride and hold him, until 1982, when Six Flags got real strict about this.

Ouch!

Susan (Waskow) Shaw, born 1967

I lived in an apartment in Affton off Mackenzie until I was like three and a half. Some of the kids at the apartments were trying to catch a dragonfly. I didn't know what a dragonfly looked like, so I caught a wasp. That is probably why I remember it, because it hurt. I caught it right on my palm.

It was probably in fourth grade. I never told anyone I was sick, because I didn't want to miss school. I had been sick for about two days, but my stomach started hurting so bad that I couldn't handle it. So I went to the nurse, and they took my temperature and told me I had a fever. But then everybody left for lunchtime and I was left alone in the nurse's office. My stomach was hurting so bad, making a groaning noise, but nobody was there to help me. And then something popped, and I immediately felt better. I don't even know how to describe it beyond that. By the time my mom got there to pick me up, I was fine. I don't know if I had an intestinal block.

Susan (Waskow) Shaw

Flicks for Kids

- *Scooby-Doo*
- *The Muppet Movie*
- *Willy Wonka and the Chocolate Factory*
- *Charlotte's Web*

Black and White Together

Kurt Walker, born 1968

The September prior to my birth, my parents moved from North City to University City. We were the second black family on my block. My family still owns the house. Next door was this family, last name Linthicum, and my dad went into business with Jack Linthicum, and they had a landscaping company for years, and they loved each other dearly. Jack went on to open up a plant nursery on Lindbergh. At the time that he opened that business, he asked my dad, "Do you want to come? We'll do it together," and my dad said, "No," because he wasn't a risk taker. "I'll just stay at Jewish Hospital, my full-time job."

Kurt Walker (left) *and his cousin Todd Patterson.*

So they ended up being great friends to the day I buried my dad a couple years ago. Jack was there. I remember growing up as a kid, we had all these pictures of family over the fireplace mantle. I'm the youngest of six siblings, so there were a lot of faces there. And there was like a little white girl with long straight hair. That was my parents' goddaughter. Her name was Hachmeister, and there was a Jewish guy my dad and my mom loved doing business with named Rosen. In my house, I saw all races of people.

Hootin' and Hollerin'

Jason Weidler, born 1971

My mom was born Catholic. My dad converted to Catholicism from Lutheranism during the early '70s. They got caught up in the charismatic movement, which was a huge spirituality movement that kind of kicked off. Many people were getting into this charismatic Christian community at the time. My brothers talked about it as being their "hippie phase," going into a deeper religious experience and expressing praise and worship with hooting and hollering in comparison with a more traditional staunch Mass that I'm more accustomed to.

They would have prayer meetings from time to time in either our home or some other couple's home. There was a community there of anywhere from twenty to thirty couples at times. And of course, the kids would all get together and play while this was all going on. They were praying in tongues and reading Bible scripture, that type of stuff, just experiencing community.

One morning I woke up, and there was the smell of breakfast being made, and bacon and eggs and all those kinds of things happening, and I kind of stumbled down into the kitchen area and saw all the charismatic people, my mom's friends, and all those couples, and then there were these other kids there that I didn't recognize. They were playing with my toys. Why are they playing with my toys? Of course, my mom was giving them something to do. We didn't know who those people were or why they were there.

It turns out, they were traveling evangelical Christian Jews that were out there spreading the word. They had a car in the driveway that had scriptures written all over it, with a big Holy Spirit bird painted on the hood. They were going from town to town. A couple that met them at church invited them over to the prayer meeting, and Mom and Dad invited them to spend the night. They just relied on God to take care of them from town to town.

POLICE
TED DREWES
FROZEN CUSTARD
Cardinals
24

The Reagan Years
1980–1989

"It's morning in America," said the ad for Ronald Reagan's re-election as president. People will debate the effect of Ronald Reagan on the country for many years, but it sure felt like morning. After Reagan's election in 1980, the country seemed to have its confidence back, after the gloom of the late 1960s and the 1970s. And when we won the Cold War at the end of the decade, it seemed like the ultimate victory. But not everybody benefited. Things didn't improve for the kids who didn't benefit from the improvements in the economy, or who lived in neighborhoods where crack cocaine led to a sharp rise in crime. But blessings still abounded for those children whose parents were caught up in this improvement in attitude and circumstance.

In St. Louis, people remember the snowstorm that brought the area to a halt at the end of January 1982. The snow was measured at 13.9 inches at Lambert Field, but as much as eighteen inches or more elsewhere. Parents growled that they couldn't get out for work for days, but kids rejoiced at all the snow days off and at all the sledding they could do. Downtown, the Gateway Mall replaced older office buildings from the Civil Courts Building. But the construction of the Gateway One building on the northern half of the block between Seventh and Eighth Street made it a half-mall. And on Grand Boulevard north of St. Louis University, a new Grand Center offered hope of a new performing arts district for the area.

Meanwhile, federal judge William Hungate issued an order in 1983 creating a Voluntary Interdistrict Transfer Program for schools in St. Louis and St. Louis County. The program was meant to use busing to fix a problem: white students overwhelmingly lived in the county. In an effort to boost minority representation in county schools, about fourteen thousand students were bused from city to county schools. About sixteen hundred county students were bused from county to city schools. Some criticized the program for making students endure long bus rides, but studies showed students transferring from the city did much better.

Whether they came from the city or the county, all kids loved one of the few true St. Louis attractions built just for kids—The Magic House in Kirkwood. The Magic House opened just before the 1980s started. Adults were allowed to tag along with the kids in a kind but condescending way, observed *Post-Dispatch* writer Elaine Viets. "Remember how you felt on Thanksgiving, when they sat you at a 'special' card table?" she wrote at the start of the 1980 Christmas season. "That's what it's like being an adult at The Magic House." As a grown-up tagging along with kids and a Brownie troop, she observed them working mechanical arms to stack gray foam blocks, a shadow wall room, computer games, and the still-popular electrostatic generator that made hair stand on end. For nothing, they could get a button showing their offspring with raised hair. It was a far cry from the musty old museums kids once endured.

So was something new called video games and personal computers. Kids got their first taste of primitive games in the 1970s, but really started loving them in the 1980s, when they began getting sophisticated. The year 1980 saw the release of the ever-addictive and ever-hungry games and computers like the Commodore 64, which was capable of handling 64 kilobytes of memory, a smidgen of what any smartphone has today. With every new product, the temptation to toss old toys aside increased.

But some toys were too strong to resist, like the Walkman, which enabled us to hear our music anywhere. The Rubik's Cube had a simple premise: mix up every part of every side and put it back together again. Only when the sides were shuffled completely did the potential puzzle shuffler realize the task was nigh impossible. That left kids shaking in their Air Jordans. The smallest kids were too busy playing with a talking teddy bear called Teddy Ruxpin or collecting their Cabbage Patch Kids dolls.

In the 1980s, there was no temptation to toss aside the St. Louis Cardinals. With feisty manager Whitey Herzog, shortstop Ozzie Smith, outfielder Vince Coleman, first baseman Jack Clark, and others, the Redbirds always played fun ball. Local kids were sure to make memories when they went to a Cardinals game in the team's pennant-winning seasons, 1982, 1985, and 1987. Those who watched the Cardinals win the World Series in 1982 will tell their grandkids about the experience. But they'll also relate with sadness their experience of watching their last St. Louis football Cardinals game before the team shipped out to Phoenix in 1988.

At home, those kids had all kinds of TV shows from which to select. *Cheers* told the story of all the characters of a bar in Boston operated by a recovering alcoholic who once pitched for the Red Sox. In a bid to show the perfect African American family, Bill Cosby starred in *The Cosby Show*, about an obstetrician and his lawyer wife raising a set of perfect kids. *Magnum P.I.* starred Tom Selleck in a crime drama set in the perfect place for any job, Hawaii. In *Family Ties*, Michael J. Fox portrayed the conservative son of 1960s hippies. Fox also showed his skill as a time traveler in the memorable flick *Back to the Future* and two more sequels. They prove going from one date to another is a bad idea, especially in a DeLorean.

With such fare, life was fairly peaceful for kids in the 1980s. It wasn't like the 1950s, but it was still good. The good times would keep going in the 1990s, but not forever.

Family Feud

Susan (Waskow) Shaw, born 1967

I was going to Kirkwood High School. My mom was teaching home ec at Webster Groves High School, and Kirkwood and Webster are big rivals. My mom was the pom-pom coordinator at Webster, and I was in the marching band at Kirkwood. There was a tradition around Thanksgiving called "Tacky Day" where you dressed up in crazy clothes to get school spirit for the big Turkey Day football game. On Tacky Day at my mom's school, she would wear my Kirkwood stuff. Then when it was our Tacky Day, I'd wear her orange and black stuff, because our rival's colors were definitely tacky. Our family Thanksgiving celebration was always at dinner, because we were busy during lunch with the Turkey Day game at noon. My mom always wrapped our turkey in foil and put it in the oven, keeping it warm until we were done cheering for our rival high school football teams.

Ice cream, yes; computers, no

In the 1980s, Goodhousekeeping.com reported, doctors told pregnant women to avoid computers and video games. They also recommended that all pregnant women should gain twenty-five to thirty pounds.

New Shoes

Darren Seals, born 1969

Darren Seals

Even though my parents had good jobs, they would pass down the shoes. By selling drugs, I had enough money to buy my own shoes. Everything was based on my shoes. I'd go out of the house with the shoes Mom gave me and look under the porch to get my own shoes. I got clothes, shoes, jewelry, girls. If you want a car, you've got to get out there and do what you need to get it. You're looking at being a freshman in high school netting $3,000 or $4,000 a month.

Once my mother did find out, she said I've got to go. I went to Northwest High School in my freshman and sophomore years and then got put out for fighting. I played baseball well, so Oakville High School accepted me as a desegregation student. I didn't sell drugs there because I felt I had a purpose. I had made Ds and Fs in the city, but I had a C average with only a couple of Ds in Oakville.

I made a few friends, who knew I was determined, and an English teacher who encouraged me. If I was still out in Oakville, I'd probably be a professional baseball player.

After high school, Darren Seals was shot 13 times in four different incidents. He mentors for his organization, Sankofa Unity Center, the St. Louis Public Schools, and the Diversion Program of the St. Louis Circuit Attorney's Office.

Country Girl Moves to the City

Valerie Schremp Hahn, born 1975, reporter, *St. Louis Post-Dispatch*

My parents built a house in Oakville in the early 1970s. Before they moved there, the land was mostly "truck farms"—for people who had small farms and trucked the produce they grew into the city to sell. It was always kind of interesting looking at the early pictures from those times, seeing nothing but fields around the house and then gradually those subdivisions would sprout up all around them. I grew up watching subdivisions being built and playing in the holes where they dug foundations and that sort of thing.

Valerie Schemp Hahn (right) *with her sister Natalie at Easter.*

My grandparents actually lived in South City just south of Tower Grove Park, so when we came into the city to visit them, it was kind of exotic. I remember driving around Arsenal Street next to Tower Grove Park looking at the buildings and thinking, "Wow, this is really neat, I want to live in a house like that one day."

And I do. I live in the Shaw neighborhood now, just north of the park, and my kids are nine and eleven. I wish they would be able to roam the streets like I did as a kid.

Who's the Smartest?

You could find the answer to that question on Saturday mornings from 1977 to 1988 on Channel 4's *D.B.'s Delight*. In it, local sixth graders vied against each other in a trivia show on such subjects as music, geography, science, and history.

Biking to Ted Drewes

Amanda (Tinnin) Duffin, born 1978

My dad did all sorts of things. He was a musician, and I do remember there was a period when I think that was all he did. He practiced a lot at home down in the basement. He was a big fan of *Night Court*, the TV show. I watched *Night Court* with him every week. One of my first experiences with a computer was playing ColecoVision. I do remember playing *Donkey Kong* with it. This was when my dad was a musician. The Smurf game looped and because it looped, one day while I was at school, my dad played until he reached 1 million points, which took hours. One summer, he dug pools with a friend. He was very thin and tan that summer. Another time he drove a truck for Lucky Trucking delivering food and supplies to Chinese restaurants. When I was fifteen, he went to work as an over-the-road truck driver.

My mom was from Dupo, Illinois. I went to elementary school at St. Anthony of Padua. I always got the impression that Mom thought it was a good education. I liked a lot of my teachers, and I liked science. That had been established for me for a long time. I liked going to Mass, liked looking at the church, the architecture, the windows, but I always found myself a little distracted during Mass itself, unfortunately. Once I was in high school, I started to see the hypocrisy.

There was a fair amount of kids in my neighborhood who were my age. I lived close enough to school and restaurants that I was able to walk or ride my bike to get around. Ted Drewes on Grand was my favorite place, and I can still remember how much I liked the hot fudge sundae. Later I graduated to the Cardinal Sin sundae with tart cherries on top.

Eyewitness to a Shooting

Ramelle "Ray" Wallace, born 1978, St. Louis police officer

In fifth grade, we lived at the corner of Clay and Penrose in North St. Louis. A lot of the drunks and drug addicts used to hang out in front of my house. And when my mother and I would come home, my mother would get tired of saying "Excuse me," to move them out of the way and would get more aggressive. "Hey, we live here, can we get into our own house?" They wound up jumping on my mother and beat her bad enough to put her in the hospital. Guys and girls, maybe about eight to ten people, jumped on my mother.

Ramelle Wallace in front of the door to the apartment where he lived in the fifth grade.

After that, they'd still come to my home, only now they'd laugh about my mother getting jumped. One of the guys who participated in the attack on my mother got into it with someone else down the street. I saw the guys, and they were angry. It was like a tussle with an older guy. The guy who helped jump my mother was in his early twenties, but the guy he was into it with was like a forty- to fifty-year-old man. Supposedly the young man had done something to the older man's daughter. I remember the conversation getting louder and louder and I heard someone scream, and then *POW!* I looked down the street, and I could see that he had a shotgun, and there was a struggle over it. The gun went off, and the younger man got shot in the face.

It was like a movie. He fell back first and smashed into the street while everybody started screaming. I remember seeing the blood and everything flying in the air. I still don't know if he lived. He got up, and a couple of his buddies kind of trotted away with him, and my mother was grabbing us and throwing us in the house.

The Fireworks Display That Wasn't

Kevin Dairaghi, born 1979

We grew up in South County, at the corner of Baptist Church Road and Lindbergh. When my parents bought our house, the area was so rural that there was only a stop light at Gravois and Baptist Church. There was a large wooded area just by our house, and I was told when I was ten I could start to explore it. But by the time that came, the wooded area had been developed into some condos and the Schnucks at Concord Village, so I never did get to explore there.

I am the youngest of five, raised in a solid Italian-Irish family. My mom was (and still is) highly active; we were always going out to different parks and activities, like the zoo, Grant's Farm, Forest Park, the Botanical Gardens, and the Arch. I didn't know until much later that we didn't have a lot of money growing up because we were still so active and always stayed busy. St Louis is great for a bunch of high-quality free or low-cost activities.

I remember one summer night, probably after watching the VP Fair, I was inspired to make some homemade fireworks. I am guessing I was eight-ish, but I invited my family, friends, neighbors, anyone I could think of, to our backyard for a cool fireworks display. They came pouring into our backyard, which seemed massive as a kid; they found seats wherever possible for the fireworks display. I was so excited, but apparently no one told me that paper, sticks, and wet flour did not make much of a display. My audience was slightly disappointed.

Making Friends

Jennifer Hughes, born 1981

I was probably two when we moved into our subdivision in Manchester, unincorporated St. Louis County. My parents were coming from Chicago and had a house built in what is now the Westbrooke Subdivision.

I don't have a whole lot of memories there as a young person. I do remember making new friends in the neighborhood, some girls who lived up the street from me. My mom and their family still keep in touch here and there. And then I had another friend, Laura, who lived down the street, and then we also made friends with the boys that lived across the street, one of whom was my age, and the other was my sister's age.

Hi Tech

Pac Man

Battlezone

Defender

Atari 2600

Atari 5200

Commodore 64

Nintendo Entertainment System

Tetris

Game Boy

Low Tech

Walkman

Air Jordans

Teddy Ruxpin

Cabbage Patch Kids dolls

A First Taste of God

David Maguire, born 1983

I think I was four or five years old, and I went out on my screened-in porch by myself. I don't remember if I sat down or knelt down, but I prayed a prayer of acceptance right there. We always were a churched family. This one parent who played guitar with my dad for children's church would dress up like a farmer, so they called him "Farmer Bruce." It was just something fun for the kids. I went to church from the time I was born, but I do vividly remember that prayer of acceptance that I prayed that day. That would be my first solid memory about the Lord. And after that, I attended Grace Christian School in Maryland Heights.

Farm Girl

Brenda Appleby, born 1984

My parents are both science teachers. They met teaching at Hazelwood West. Because my dad was a teacher, we were able to go on long summer trips every year. One of the places we went to was the farm where our grandparents lived in central Kansas. My dad grew up there. Our grandparents moved to town when I was in first grade, but my earliest memories are of driving from St. Louis to visit them on the farm. My grandma had this huge garden all around the house, and of course, when you're that little, the flowers are right at your eye level. It was like a jungle for us. We'd have our wading pool set up in the middle of the yard with the garden all around it, and that well water was very, very cold.

We would set up a bucket with water next to the pool, so that when you were going into the pool, you could rinse the grass clippings off your feet before getting into the water. It was always a lot of fun to be there. There was a big, big bell hanging on a post. They used to use it to call people in from the fields for dinner. Of course, with kids and a giant bell, you're going to be ringing the bell a lot.

ST. LOUIS

Into the Future
1990–1999

Americans got used to quiet and prosperity in the 1990s, the decade after the fall of communism and before the 9/11 attacks. Republicans and Democrats fought like never before, and President Bill Clinton became only the second president in history to be impeached. People thought the turn of the computer clocks from December 31, 1999, to January 1, 2000, would unleash online Armageddon. The promised disaster never came, but there was plenty of opportunity for one to happen in the new millennium.

Locally, the Great Flood of 1993 raised the rivers to levels not seen since human beings began keeping records. That same year, St. Louisans took their first ride on MetroLink, a light rail system that promised to connect much of the region. Freeman Bosley Jr. became the first black mayor of St. Louis and lost to the second black mayor, Clarence Harmon. At the end of the century, it was a sign of forward but incomplete movement in the economic fortunes of African Americans. More black teenagers attended school, while the number of blacks in professional and management jobs skyrocketed. But many lived in poverty and crime-ridden neighborhoods.

Black or white, the 1990s were not a time for kids who savored trips to the World Series. The Cardinals only made it to the National League Championship Series once, in 1996, and lost to the Atlanta Braves in seven games. But the home team offered kids plenty of the stuff that makes memories. The 1996 team was the first under the helm of the legendary manager Tony LaRussa. The next year, Mark McGwire came to the team and started swatting the kind of home runs that everyone remembers for a lifetime. In 1998, he smashed seventy home runs, burying Roger Maris's record of sixty-one set in 1961. Only later did the hometowners learn that McGwire had help from steroids. But by that time, they were talking about how quarterback Kurt Warner led the new St. Louis Rams to victory in the 1999 Super Bowl.

Kids who didn't like sports had a new choice when the City Museum opened in 1997. Owner Bob Cassilly stuffed the place with things a kid would install, like caves, a five-story slide, the MonstroCity Jungle Gym, and a school bus hanging over the edge of a roof. A six thousand square foot section within the City Museum contained Bill Christman's Museum of Mirth, Mystery and Mayhem. Grown-ups might grouse that none of it makes sense. But it makes sense to kids because it was designed like a kid would design it.

The 1990s were the years the computers mattered for real. The Internet turned the computer from a cute device for playing video games and writing term papers to something that brought the whole world into the house. But it wasn't like it is today. It came through dial-up on phone lines, a jarring combination of dialing sounds, whizzes, static, whines, dings, and other noises that sometimes did and sometimes didn't connect you to the World Wide Web. Connections were a crawl compared to today's rocket fast links. We got excited when we heard the words "You've Got Mail." You couldn't stay on for long, because nobody else could use the phone while we were online. By today's standards, it was primitive. But this was a revolution that changed the world.

As computers truly became useful in the 1990s, cable television also became a force. It provided vastly more entertainment selections, but also cut into the shared experiences when viewers only had three networks from which to choose. Cable networks started producing original content, but not always suitable for young children. *Beavis and Butt-Head* and *South Park* were hardly the kind of cartoons most parents wanted their kids to watch. Neither was another cartoon on free TV, *The Simpsons.* For parents who didn't want their kids to see such content, Congress passed a law in 1996 mandating the installation of V-chips in new TVs. With the chips, parents could screen programs they thought were improper. But movies didn't have V-chip, and parents could only hope that their teens would stay away from flicks rated "R."

It was more likely in the 1990s that only one parent would screen the television or movie selections. Around one child in five in the 1990s lived only with his or her mother. It was one of many changes families and kids had to deal with as they prepared to move the clock from the second millennium to the third.

Some worried disaster might come from that change. They noted that early computers with tiny memories saved space by referring to years with two digits rather than four. That was fine in years starting with "19," they said. They worried a switch from December 31, 1999, to January 1, 2000, might confuse computers and cause everything from electrical power to insurance companies to stop. Nothing happened at 12:01 a.m. on January 1, 2000, proving the Y2K scare was a needless worry.

But there was much to worry about in the years after that, starting with man-made global warming and other environmental challenges and moving down to simple war and hatred. Science fiction, particularly the *Star Trek* movies and TV shows, gave the impression that people of the twentieth and twenty-first century eventually would solve those problems and move into the galaxy. The astounding advances of the previous century made it appear that they could.

As the century ended, there was not the sense of excitement like what greeted the start of the twentieth century. One indication of what might be ahead happened on April 20, 1999, when two teenagers killed thirteen and injured more than twenty more at Columbine High School in Colorado. But nobody had an inkling of the kind of violence a relatively unknown Saudi Arabian terrorist leader named Osama bin Laden was plotting.

Hailing the New Home Run King

Victoria (Vicki) Ann Tissot Mikow, born 1981

I worked at the Magic House for about seven years. I started in high school, all through college, and then a little after I graduated from college. On a summer night when we were at a meeting or cleaning afterwards, we put the Cardinals game on, blasting over the intercom. The night he was going to break the record, we knew Mark McGwire was going to hit No. 62. I just knew it. And when he did, my manager went and grabbed a bunch of waxed paper, and we slid down the slide—that three-story slide—on wax paper. We did it really fast.

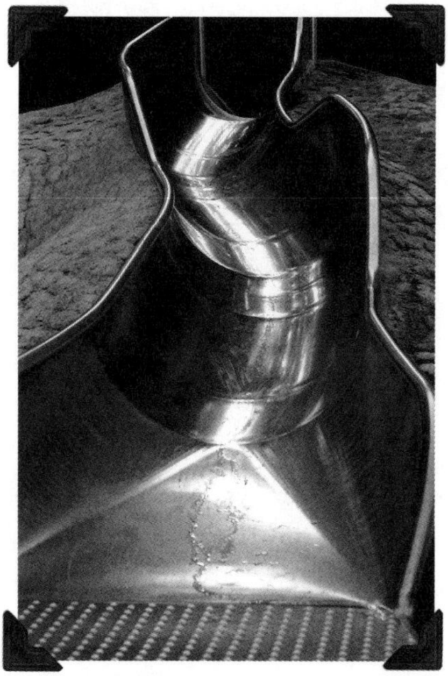

High schools that closed in the 1990s

Smith Academy, 1992

St. Louis Health Care Program High School, 1992

St. Louis Academy of International Language and Studies, 1993

Northwest High School, 1993

From As to Fs

David Maguire, born 1983

Grace Christian School in Maryland Heights where I went to elementary school was a very sheltered environment. It was a small school with just over three hundred kids. Classes would be anywhere from high teens to high twenties, making for a pretty close, tight-knit environment. Right around eleven or twelve years of age, I became a little bit rebellious. My motives probably had something to do with it, because I didn't want to be told what to do. So I started poking holes in doctrine. I would make my sticking point something that was pretty petty. For instance, there were different dress codes for boys and girls. Boys weren't allowed to have long hair a certain length, and I took issue with that. I was leaning more and more toward not seeking the Lord, toward doing my own thing.

After seventh grade, I left that school and started going to Nipher Middle School in Kirkwood. I started dipping my toes in the devil's water and started smoking cigarettes, smoking pot, going to parties, and drinking beer here and there when I could get my hands on it, which was kind of few and far between. I was a new kid at school, and didn't know a lot of people, so the opportunities weren't there. Once I hit the freshman year of high school, it was just full blown partying. I dropped out my sophomore year. I went from being a straight A student to dropping out because I had no desire to do it anymore.

Dollar Night at the Avalon

Joseph Sedberry, born 1983, assistant manager, QuikTrip

Joseph Sedberry with his mom, Paula.

I went to Kennard, and then I went to McKinley. Both were gifted schools that required me to take IQ tests to get in. I went to Gateway High School after that. I did really good at Kennard and McKinley. When I got to high school, I was almost overprepared. I had straight As in freshman year. Gateway just didn't have the curriculum that would challenge me. I got pretty bored after freshman year because I had to start taking senior classes, and I eventually dropped out because it was just too boring for me.

I used to go to the Avalon Theater down Christy all the time with my friends. We'd walk or ride our bikes since it's not too far, only about a mile. I saw whatever was showing, dollar movies, action movies, R-rated movies—it didn't matter. I saw *Jurassic Park* there when it was only a dollar. We probably took it from my parents or something as I recall. We got allowances, like five bucks a week.

Flicks

Groundhog Day	*Edward Scissorhands*
Jurassic Park	*Pretty Woman*
Titanic	

Mixed Marriage

Andrea Johnson, born 1984

My mom is white, and my dad is black. They met in Connecticut in Hartford, and my mom was there to go to college, and my dad had moved there because his sister had moved there. I believe they lived in the same apartment building, and that's how they met. It took my mom's family some time to get used to it.

Definitely kids would make comments, like "You're being black today," or "You're being white today." What was difficult was that I didn't look like my mom at all. The neighborhoods I grew up in were pretty white. After early elementary school, it wasn't really a thing.

Andrea Johnson

TV Shows

Seinfeld

Dawson's Creek

Friends

Felicity

Buffy the Vampire Slayer

Bikes in the Suburbs

Sarah Baraba, born 1987

There were like four streets that were connected as a square near my home. We'd ride our bikes in the streets and could walk to our backyards. People's backyards butted up to each other. It was the kind of neighborhood where you would have been able to go out and roam as a kid.

We got a computer about '98, but we didn't get the internet until several years later. We had games, lots of educational software. Even the games that we had were all educational.

Kiddie Movies

Toy Story

Beauty and The Beast

Lion King

Aladdin

Jumanji

Home Alone

Black and White in Ferguson

Peter M. Guth, born 1987

There were lots of white families and a few black families in the neighborhood. That was the dynamic I remember, at least for trick-or-treating. Growing up, I had two main best friends. One of them was white, and the other one was black. Especially when I moved there, there was a lot of playing outside, playing superheroes. We felt at that time like we had that neighborhood to ourselves.

Watching an Uncle Die

Kristin (Woehr) du Bruyn, born 1988

I remember him being in a wheelchair suffering from ALS, and I remember him not being able to talk, so he had to use that little computerized voice. We would visit my aunt a lot. I also remember going into the living room in the morning. My mom had the cord phone, and she was crying, and I asked what was wrong, and she said my uncle had died. He had died in his sleep. He was my mom's sister's husband. He died in his bed. That freaked me.

Kristin (Woehr) du Bruyn

A Creek in Crestwood

Annemarie Nauert, born 1988

The majority of my friends that I palled around with lived in my neighborhood in Crestwood. We would cut through our neighbors' yards, go up to their house and see if they were home almost every day after school. I lived in that neighborhood until I was in third grade. Every day after school, we would pretty much spend the daylight hours together, and we had elaborate imaginary games that we had devised that kept us pretty busy. In the summer, I know we spent the majority of the day exploring the creek in the Crestwood Park, climbing trees, playing games. We would spend hours and hours in that creek exploring.

I think we were really lucky that we were just old enough to have a childhood free from screens and electronic devices. I did not play or see a video game until I was twelve and saw it at my cousin's house. I also never watched Saturday morning cartoons. I think we were very sheltered from that kind of screen time. My parents just encouraged getting outside and playing with our friends. I had piano lessons, but honestly, it didn't chew up that much time. Mostly, it was very unstructured, go out and play.

Annemarie (middle row, second from right)

Outside of Marriage

Among girls fifteen to nineteen, the birth rate for unmarried women jumped from 7 per 1,000 in 1940 to 46 per 1,000 in 1994.

Watching McGwire Hit Number 62

Madison Hayes, born 1988

Every time he'd come up to bat, of course, everyone would stand up. When he finally hit that one, a couple of people around us started sitting down, thinking it would just be a fly out. It was a good thing they did because the only reason I got to see it is because the guy in front of us sat down. It just nudged over left field. It was one of the loudest times I've ever been in Busch Stadium. It was all fairly standard to have the fireworks and everybody cheering.

Rooted in Kinloch

Kiarra Lynn Smith, born 1989

My mother grew up in Kinloch. Her grandmother, who is my great-grandmother, moved to Kinloch in the 1920s from Arkansas. I think it was during the Great Migration. My father grew up in University City. He's black, but his ancestors came from Italy at the turn of the century to Missouri. I'm an only child. A portion of my early childhood was spent between Kinloch and the Central West End on Lindell.

Kiarra Lynn Smith

I was probably about six when I moved out of Kinloch. All of my family had grown up in Kinloch. But by the time I came along, there were not that many people left in Kinloch. It had basically deteriorated. I mainly played with my cousins because they were always where we were. I had one cousin, C.C. I had more, but the main one I played with was C.C. What really hurt things was when the airport bought land in Kinloch. They bought my great-grandmother's house, where we had lived. They tore it down and my family used the money we got to move to Ferguson.

My mother sold hair products to all the beauty shops and barber colleges throughout St. Louis. She also worked for different nonprofits. My mother is very religious, and our lives were spent in the church.

The Family Translator

Andrej Dzidic, born 1993

Andrej Dzidic was two when his parents brought him to St. Louis from Sarajevo, Bosnia, in 1995.

We had five dollars to our name when we came to the United States. My uncle and a few cousins lived here, but I was an only child. My dad worked for the St. Louis Ambush, playing professional soccer. In Bosnia, he played for Zeljo, one of two professional soccer teams in Sarajevo. He played from 1995-96 here. After that, he needed a job that would provide insurance, so he started working for a factory that made plastic bags. My mom started working for this company that makes jerseys for the Cardinals, Blues, and Rams. My dad's Catholic and my mom's Muslim, but neither of my parents are religious.

My parents were big on school, and as a result I was in the gifted program since kindergarten at Bernard Elementary School. I was really shy growing up. My best friend, we've been friends since seven or eight years old, is Serbian. At home, you speak your native language and try to maintain the culture, but at school, you try and assimilate. Part of you always feels like you stick out a little bit, but it's always a blessing that you're a different culture.

For my parents, I translated anything, from going into cell phone stores, going into any store, really, parent, teacher conferences. Every time we had to order food, from the time I was six. Whenever they would order, they would point at it. Otherwise, I would translate. My mom speaks worse, but understands English better. My dad speaks it better, but understands it worse. I remember my mom became a family friend's godmother. Instead of saying "godmother," she called herself "mother of God."

TED DREWES
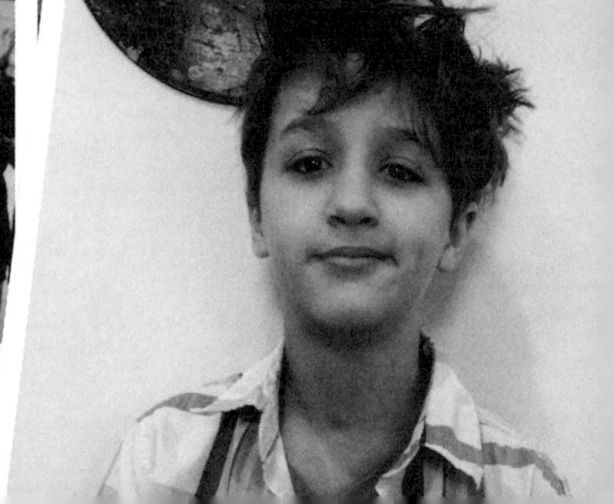

Brave New World 2000–2019

The 2000s started in peace but turned violent when terrorists commandeered four airliners and used them as missiles in attacks that killed thousands and changed the world. The events of September 11, 2001, reminded everyone of the dangers of the new millennium. In the years that followed, the United States found itself in wars without end in Afghanistan and Iraq. The second President Bush started them, and President Barack Obama sought to bring those wars under control. Then came Donald Trump, who shook things up with his unique style.

In this region, the City of St. Louis kept losing population and, in some years, gained the unwelcome "honor" of having the greatest number of murders per thousand of any large city. Locals said that was because St. Louis had a smaller portion of its metropolitan area than other big cities and that much of the city consists of high-crime areas. That didn't reassure people elsewhere. The area's racial tensions broke out in the open in August 2014, when a white police officer shot and killed an unarmed black man named Michael Brown in the North County suburb of Ferguson. The protests brought worldwide attention and led to an overdue region-wide examination of the legal and institutional causes of racial injustice. The 2000s also saw a winding down of the transfer programs in which thousands of African American students attended county schools. Black students from the city often did better in county schools, but even better in magnet schools in the city.

The poverty rate among African Americans declined from 34.7 to 21.4 percent, in the period, but was still 2.5 times as high as whites. And the rate of incarceration was more than six times as much as whites. "Forward Through Ferguson: A Path Toward Racial Equity," a report issued after the Michael Brown shooting, noted that the life expectancy in mostly white suburban Wildwood was more than ninety-one but less than fifty-six in mostly black Kinloch. It made a long list of recommendations for police reform. In schools, its list of suggestions included dealing with hunger, providing health services, and moving against unconscious bias. At the start of the twenty-first century, young African Americans have greater economic opportunities and are free from the blatant racism their great-great grandparents faced. But significant barriers to equity among the races still exist.

Whether they were black or white, kids started making baseball memories in a new location in 2006, when the Cardinals moved into a new stadium. They were in the playoffs twelve times from 2000 to 2015 and won the World Series three times. The Rams left St. Louis and returned to Los Angeles. Not to worry, because St. Louis got a Major League Soccer team in 2019. Kids had plenty to "ooh" and "aah" about when Citygarden opened downtown in 2009, complete with a huge disembodied metal head on its side and bunches of squirting water fountains to run through and get soaked. And visitors had their first look at a stunning $380 million makeover of the Gateway Arch grounds and museum in 2018.

Local kids who experienced this got a good education, but not always. The St. Louis Public School system struggled with poor management and lost its state accreditation for a while. But city residents had another choice of where to send their youngsters. Charter schools operated without many of the rules that some said hamstrung traditional public schools. Questions remained whether the schools were better, but the Missouri Charter Public Schools Association listed thirty-eight of them in St. Louis in 2019. Wherever students attended, scares about school shootings didn't help their studies. School districts took expensive steps to secure their buildings. A large part of a $105 million bond issue in the Lindbergh Schools in 2019, for example, was for making it harder for shooters to invade Lindbergh High School and other district buildings. Meanwhile, at Lindbergh and elsewhere, school boards worked to ensure that all students had access to technology unknown a few years earlier.

In numerous ways, kids of the 2000s were in a vastly different world than their parents and grandparents. Interracial marriage is taken as normal. Same-sex marriages in which spouses have rights to adopt may not have the same degree of public acceptance. But the Supreme Court's 2015 ruling that all states must accept it has changed the views of many on the practice. It's one way the world of today's kids is vastly different from the days of their grandparents. For many parents, the structured play date replaced unsupervised play with any kid who was available in the neighborhood. And the Centers for Disease Control and Prevention reported in 2016 that one out of twenty children took medicine for attention deficit/hyperactivity disorder.

These different practices are just two of the many changes that have occurred that have nothing to do with the advance of technology. Shakespeare easily could have had the kids of the 2000s in mind when he penned the words "O brave new world, that has such people in't." Generation Z—born from 1995 to 2015—is far removed from earlier generations. James Emery White wrote the book *Meet Generation Z: Understanding and Reaching the New Post-Christian World.* He says the Generation Z is more racially diverse. They're more at home with technology than their parents. Large numbers have no religious affiliation. They are more willing to accept the LGBTQIA+ community and depend more on word of mouth information than big media. They are mature, anxious to go to work, have short attention spans, and think spatially and in 4D. They are less active and often are obese.

If it seems like the children of the 2000s have gone through a lot, kids always have survived disruption. Those in this book lived in one small part of a world that experienced racist mobs, poverty, war, and so much more. They grew up knowing that at any time atomic bombs could destroy the world. Yet they survived. They made friends and imagined the mud pies they'd made were castles. They endured abuse and tragedy or lived around loving parents who filled their lives with happy events. As adults, they carried their memories of childhood with them, for better or worse. Kids today face disaster in global climate change, wars, and an exploding world population. Still, whatever else they're experiencing, kids today still act like kids. As long as they do that, there's hope for those growing up in the third millennium.

Death Came Suddenly

Jennifer Hughes, born 1981

My dad and I were really close. He passed away when I was 18, in March of my senior year of high school. My sister and I were at a concert, and he and my mom were on the way to pick us up. He had a heart attack, I think right in the parking lot. He was transported to the hospital and didn't make it. I came home, nobody was there, which was really unusual. Then my mom came home with her best friend. After she walked in the door, and he wasn't with her, I already knew what had happened.

Fighting for Kerry

Sarah Baraba, born 1987

I wasn't allowed to spend a lot of time on the computer because it was dial up. I was only able to squeeze in at least an hour a day. My parents would always check my e-mail, but I didn't do anything risqué, being a very busy and involved student.

I played volleyball all four years of high school, was in the National Honor Society, and played violin in the orchestra. I was one of the student board members for the safe-driving Reaching Adolescent Driver, or RAD, group because there had been several student fatalities from car crashes while I was at Lindbergh. It was not "rad" at all, though—it was very nerdy.

In 2004, we started a group called "Students for Kerry" and it turned into the Lindbergh Liberal Union. There was another group called the Young Republicans, who were on the opposite side of the political spectrum. The students who were involved in these groups were very vocal. We plastered the campus with posters. They eventually didn't allow it.

The Attack on 9/11

Kiarra Lynn Smith, born 1989

In August 2001, I was on an airplane. And I said, "I'm afraid the airplane will crash into a building." The lady next to me said, "Planes don't crash into buildings." On 9/11, I stopped watching TV because they kept showing the planes crashing into the Twin Towers over and over and over, and it made me depressed. On the television, they wouldn't stop showing it. No matter what station I turned to, it was on.

The New Family

From 1960 to 2016, the percentage of American children in two-parent households dropped from 88 percent to 69 percent.

From 1960 to 2012, the percentage of dual income households jumped from 25 percent to 60 percent.

Not a Dungeon

Aodhan La Croix, born 1998

Everyone always thinks homeschoolers are sequestered away, like in some kind of dungeon and never get out at all. No, the homeschoolers always go hang out with each other on nice days, because they finish their work by 10:30, because they got up at 6, did it all, and then they all go to parks. The Science Center counted as a field trip. There are a lot of great things about being homeschooled. I probably did miss out on experiences, but from what I've heard, they're not experiences I wanted to have.

Talking Religion at Webster Groves High School

Alison Vedova, born 1999

Alison Vedova

I've been going to church, I believe, my whole life. It's definitely not something that people talk about at school. One of my close friends is a Christian, actually a few of them, but it's not brought up at school.

I've never done stuff like drugs. I don't hang out with the wrong people, or I guess it's more like people that make wrong decisions. I've always been taught not to do those things.

I know that things will always work out. There's someone there for me. I know that one day I'll get married, and one day I'll have children. I just know now that what happens isn't always going to be. That being said, I do worry a lot. It runs in my family. It's not really intense, it's more like, "This could happen."

It really is good, guys and gals

Everybody knows Ted Drewes is the first choice of St. Louisans who want a cold treat. But if your kids are persnickety, you may want to have them decide in advance before you bring them there to celebrate their graduation from kindergarten. Amidst the concretes, malts, shakes, sundaes, floats, and ice cream sodas, the on-line menu lists twenty-two specials and favorites, along with thirty-nine toppings and add-ons. Among the specialties are Crater Copernicus, Dutchman, Cinna-Crunch, and Orange Slushy. Pecan, Tart Cherry, and Heath Bar lead the list of toppings and add-ons. Don't forget to ask them to turn your concrete over for you.

Homecoming Queen

Tabitha (Tabby) Stowers, born 2000

When I became Kirkwood's homecoming queen on November 4, 2017, I was really excited to think I would be queen. We share our homecoming game with Webster Groves High School. I actually ordered my dress online. My mom helped me. It was a black dress with a line of jewels around the neck.

I'll sometimes use my phone in class, but that's only if I have free time if I do all my work in class. I text like every day. How often? Probably like every five minutes.

Being mixed race is interesting because I feel like I'm torn sometimes with situations that happen in St. Louis. It feels like I have to pick sides all the time. Sometimes me and my dad have talks. He's told me to be cautious. I know we've gotten pulled over before for having dark license plates. He says that the reason he got pulled over is because he's African American. Everyone's been pretty accepting of me, especially at school, because there are a lot of mixed race kids at my school, too.

Tabitha Stowers

Time on the phone

The average American teen exchanged about 30 text messages a day during 2015, the Pew Research Center reported. The center said 88 percent of teens have access to smartphones or cell phones. Of those, 90 percent exchange texts. Of the teens surveyed, 71 percent said they use Facebook. Instagram is next, followed by Snapchat.

A Child of Indian Immigrants in Chesterfield

Vindhya Yanamadala, born 2000

My parents grew up in a state called Andhra Pradesh in South India. We go back to India to visit around every two years. It's definitely very different, the culture and the way the people live. My dad came here for college, and my mom came here for her residency after she married my dad. My dad is a psychiatrist, and my mom's an OB/GYN. It was an arranged marriage, and they met for the first time at my aunt's wedding.

I was involved in a lot until around fourth grade: tennis, gymnastics, ice skating. One thing that I still continue to this day is ice skating. I've had voice lessons since I was four. I think I was fairly active, fairly busy as a child. For ice skating, we would go to St. Louis Mills mall. For tennis, we would go to Gravois Bluffs, to Sunset Tennis Center. That was something my brother and I did. I took Indian classical and western musical class. I took gymnastics once a week, more for fun. That was from first to fourth grade. It was my mom who kind of made the decision to stop. I was kind of stressed all the time, and time management was becoming a hard thing with all the activities.

A Forever Change

Treveon Pittman, born 2004

Life was kind of rough for me. Then my grandfather told me about Jesus. He's the Savior. If it wasn't for Him, I wouldn't be on this earth. He died for my sins and rose three days later. I feel a lot better. I know that God is right here with me, and where I go, He's right here with me.

A Child of Refugees Discovers Her Identity

Waamene Wifa, born 2004

I grew up in St. Louis. My parents moved from Nigeria to the United States, and then they had me a year later. I was just kind of trying to figure out who I am, because I couldn't really classify myself. I wasn't all the way American, but I wasn't all the way Nigerian, so what was I? Where did I fit in? I really didn't think I was much of anything, but my parents always told me that just because you're from Nigeria, that doesn't mean you're not special. And just because you grew up in America doesn't make you anything less. You are who you are, Nigerian American, and you should be proud.

Growing up with refugee, immigrant parents really makes you want to work harder when you are in the United States because they are constantly reminding you that they went through a lot in their country to get here. If I come back with a grade lower than a B, it's over.

Waamene Wifa

Her Brother Almost Died

Aurora Kenner, born 2006

When I was six, my brother had systemic strep and toxic shock in his hip. The hospital said if we'd have kept him home, he would have died. I was kind of oblivious to what was going on, because I was so young, but what I did understand freaked me out. For like a year, I did have dreams about it, and I do try to appreciate him more.

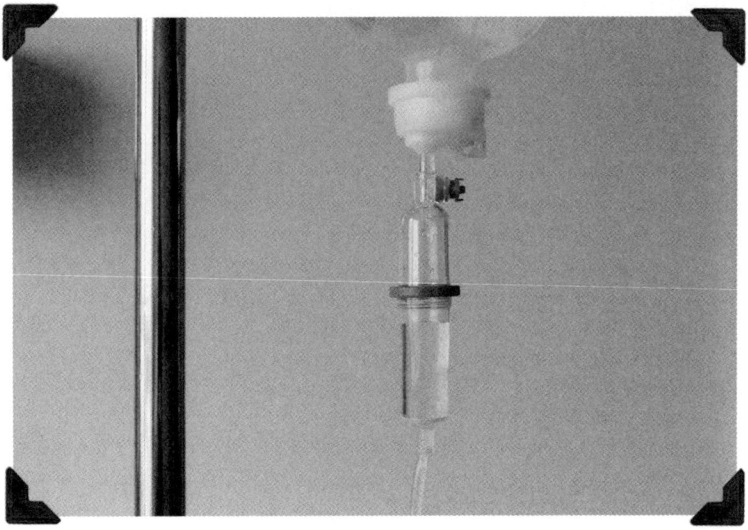

Solution: Less homework

Sixth grade school backpacks tested in New York City schools in 2009 weighed an average of 18.4 pounds, books and all. Some weighed as much as 30 pounds. Kids shouldn't carry more than 10 to 20 percent of their weight on their backs, the American Academy of Pediatrics said.

A Nine-Year Old Looks at Life

Milo Marston, born 2008 (interviewed in 2017)

My favorite subject was math by far. There's a lot to find out about it. I like how you can take one statement and transform it into something completely different. I'd like to be a physicist or a mathematician eventually. I like the Magic House, the Science Center, and the Planetarium. I just went to the Book Fair and got a book by Neil deGrasse Tyson.

I have classmates who are friends and two or three friends in the neighborhood, but I actually don't usually get together with them often. I prefer to read fiction books like *Harry Potter*. I like Disney and Pixar, although I'm not that big of a *Star Wars* fan. I like taking trips to the beach on summer vacation and playing the flute. In flute practice, I'm working on "Ode to Joy."

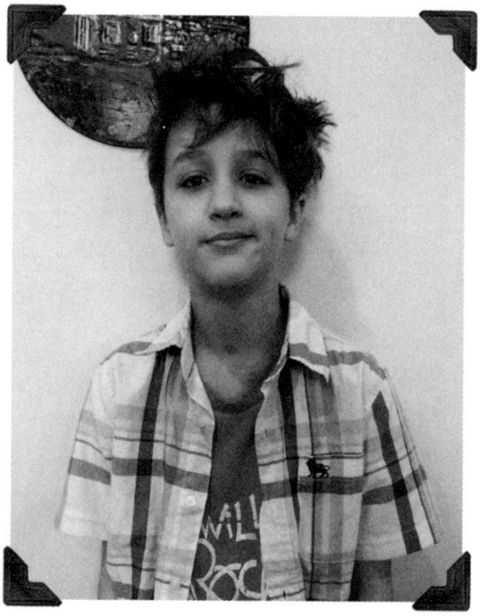

Milo Marston

I don't have a phone, even though a lot of my friends do. It's not that big a deal, to be honest. I think it's pretty amazing how much we've progressed over the past few decades, and it makes me optimistic about the future. But I do worry about the environment and greenhouse gases.

I'd describe myself as thoughtful. I have a sister, Molly. She's three, but she always says she's three and a half. We have a love-hate relationship.

The future? Hopefully, not very greenhouse gassy.

Epilogue: My Life as a Country Boy

Jim Merkel

For sheer chaos, few places in St. Louis County match Manchester Road at Interstate 270. The West County Center, numerous strip stores, office buildings, and a mass of suburban homes in all directions combine to bring more many thousands of vehicles a day to Manchester just east of I-270. Traffic is so great that eastbound and westbound lanes of Manchester west of the interstate separate, creating an island surrounded by congestion. People in the stores and the Marcus Des Peres 14 Cinema go about their business in the midst of the roar of vehicles just a two-minute walk away. But not that long ago, it was quiet, almost rural. I know, because I once lived in a house that today is within that island.

We moved there in the summer of 1956, with my oldest sister Lois and my older brother Charles, around my fifth birthday. Home was a one-story ranch house with white metal siding and an adjoining two-vehicle carport on a dead-end street on the north side of Manchester Road. To the east, the Manchester Drive-In showed movies on the present site of West County Center. Behind our house was a barbed wire fence topped by an electrified wire, formidable enough to keep horses inside and big folks out. But I could crawl under it and wander through what seemed like miles of trees and fields. In time, I discovered a quarry, perfect for sneaking in with a friend and hearing the immortal words, "Hey, you kids, get out of here!" I was on my own, to imagine all sorts of wonders.

School intervened, and I attended kindergarten in the Mason Ridge Elementary School on South Mason Road next to the current route of Interstate 64. My teacher, Gretchen L. Kilpatrick, wrote in my report card that "Jimmy has been a pleasure to have. His sense of humour (sic) has pepped us all up at times. He tries hard and is a good little worker," But she offered a warning: "He should work on his 'scatterbrain' forgetfulness though." Nothing's changed. I'm still scatterbrained, and I still need to work on that forgetfulness.

In first grade, the nuns at St. Clement Catholic School in Des Peres had to figure out what to do with me, because my parents were Catholic, and good Catholic parents sent their kids to Catholic school. I paid great attention when the nuns instructed me in the ways of the Catholic Church, including confession and communion. I wasn't sure whether my sins were sufficient for my first confession, so I stole a nickel pack of chewing gum from a store to make sure.

I did my real learning during recess. I learned how nasty budding bullies can be. I learned lessons in human relations that I'll keep all my life. I discovered how to fight and learned that what grownups tell you isn't always the truth. One day, for example, I overheard a classmate say there is no Santa Claus and immediately decided he was right. My mother tried to dissuade me, but I was convinced.

I knew my parents and not a guy in an airborne sleigh provided late-December gifts, but that didn't ease my greed for everything I could get on Christmas. The holiday started on Christmas Eve, when my father finally looked for a tree. By that time, the lots were stripped of anything worthy of being called a "tree," but after much fiddling, it actually looked decent when he planted it in our living room. Winter gripped the area for months after Christmas and provided many opportunities to use our sleds. Maybe a half-mile to the west, I found the greatest slope, just right for an exhilarating ride, except for the bottom. For there flowed an icy creek. Those who directed their sleds in the right direction found their way across a small bridge. But, I missed that bridge once and found myself drenched in polar water. I was more blessed, but still frigid, when we visited Kirkwood Park to ice skate on a parking lot that had been drenched with water that quickly froze. My bones shook as I slid across the ice. Soon I was close to a fire in a trash barrel near the parking lot with hot chocolate meant to ease the chill.

The outdoors was our living room on warmer days. At night, we stood in the backyard and watched a satellite pass over. At mealtime, Mom called us in with a whistle. She smoked and wasn't much of a housekeeper. But she loved and encouraged me, and I'll always love her for that. She demonstrated in the TV set controversy that she could get what she wanted. Dad said he wouldn't allow us to have a TV until my tenth birthday, in June 1961, which was too long for Mom to wait. Mom's chance came when Dad got a used set in a trade-in for a piano. The TV went in the basement, where we spent Sunday nights watching *Have Gun Will Travel* and *Gunsmoke.*

In third grade, I returned to Mason Ridge, where my world widened. On the school bus, somebody organized a vote between Kennedy and Nixon for president. Nixon won easily. Then the school offered a Russian language class. I learned one word in this Cold War era class: *dasvidaniya*, or "goodbye." I said that word when we moved away from Des Peres to a house near my dad's piano store in Webster Groves in 1961. I was halfway through fourth grade, no longer a kid, but a person on the edge of that strange time called adolescence. My new life would be more complicated, darker, and more full of potential. My memories changed from black and white to color. But my sparse memories of Des Peres are in some ways superior. They offer enough detail to watch a five-year-old boy—this boy—crawl under a barbed wire fence to explore the trees and the fields beyond.

Notes and Acknowledgments: How I Wrote This Book

Jim Merkel

When I started this project in January 2017, I didn't realize what a monster it would become. It turned into by far the most difficult of the five books I've written about St. Louis. It was my longest project, which means I often wondered whether it would ever be done. That means, naturally, that my list of people to thank is longer. I'll start with the local coffee shops and restaurants where I met many of the more than 110 people I interviewed and recorded for this book. Also at those places, I made phone calls and wrote. There's nothing like the atmosphere of a coffee house to open up an interview subject and to get words flowing. It's just more fun.

Finding those subjects wasn't fun. Trying to find people with an even mix of ages, sexes, races, and personal interests isn't easy. Neither is stepping way out and approaching somebody. Imagine approaching strangers who are nothing like you and asking them if they would mind being grilled about personal details of their childhood. I got my share of nos and yeses, which turned into nos when a person stood me up for an appointment. I don't blame them. I respect them, actually. On the other hand, I love those who took a chance and now are in the book I've written.

I found them in all kinds of ways, including walking up to someone with green hair at a fair and asking for an interview. Some were relatives or friends of relatives and friends. Some came from my church or a request through Facebook. I also called PR people—anybody, really—to ask for help. In a few cases, I don't know how I got linked up. About twenty-five of them came from the St. Louis Public Library. I spent four Saturdays in October 2017 at different branches of that library finding them. St. Louis Public Library Auditorium Coordinator Joe Schwartz put the out word that people might get in a book if they showed up on one of those Saturdays and talked to me about their experience growing up in St. Louis. From the first Saturday to the last, they didn't disappoint. Their stories were marvelous and provided a perspective that I probably wouldn't have found elsewhere. What a joy to meet so many different kinds of people, all with their own stories and adventures, as you'd expect from people who would answer an appeal to tell the story of their childhood to an author writing a book.

I'm happy to say that many of the people I interviewed became personal friends. Eighteen of them met me for lunch one Sunday afternoon in late March 2019 at CJ Muggs in downtown Webster Groves to catch up and tell their stories again. The tales of these eighteen individuals were amazingly different.

On such a day, I loved hearing how all of these different people lived. But my stories aren't complete without the help of research institutions that give the background of why children acted the same way in a certain era. My essays with each of the ten time periods provided some important context. All of them required significant research. In the St. Louis Room of the St. Louis Public Library's Central Library downtown and the Missouri Historical Society's Library & Research Center I regularly found anecdotes and detailed research material that fleshed out my stories. The century-old clippings and microfilm files of old newspapers at the Central

Library always gave me the details I needed. So did the yellowing record books on its shelves and its marvelous collection of books on St. Louis history.

The extensive collection of old magazines, oral histories, and odds and ends that all researchers crave at the Historical Society's Library & Research Center added to the stack of statistics and stories I had to use. Part of my work on each chapter included spending time at both places. The Internet is a good place to start, but anybody who says it'll take the place of visits to libraries like the ones I mentioned is wrong. One source I came to love was the online *St. Louis Post-Dispatch* which offers every article that the paper has printed since 1870s. The service, offered by Newspapers.com, enabled me to spend more time at home rather than spend evenings at the Central Library searching through microfilm.

My thanks go to Josh Stevens at Reedy Press, my editor and publisher for this project. I can't forget Barb Northcott, who always turns my scribbles into the handsome books you buy, along with the copyeditors, proofreaders, and designers who make it elegant. Thanks to Don Korte, the Reedy Press jack-of-all-trades, who consistently does his best at every task Josh gives him. Then there's Mischelle Leahy, who sells the books into the stores and online outlets, and Joel Carter, who manages our new warehouse. And thanks to Calvin Riley for his invaluable insight into the area's African American community.

If the final product makes your day, you've made mine. The idea that you'd get enjoyment out of something I wrote is much greater pay than I'll ever get from selling these books. That keeps me writing. Bless you, all of you, who tell me that at a book signing or speech. I'll thank God for that, but most of all, I'll thank Him for my faithful wife, Lorraine. She was always faithful, always ready to proofread. Too often, I've abandoned her so I can write these words. In spite of that, she stays near me, always encouraging, always loving.

I'll always thank Lorraine more than anyone else. But after her, I'll thank everyone who allowed me to tell their stories. Rich or poor, black or white, known and unknown, they opened up with stories about their life. Their tales were amazing, because everybody has stories to tell about their lives. I know I've left certain groups out. But I also believe I've done a pretty good job of balancing the sexes, races, and peoples of the times, from 1900 to the present.

Finally, here's something amazing. One of the first people I interviewed for the book was Dorothy (Danner) Hunter. She was born in 1907 and spent her childhood in the 3800 block of Connecticut Street, south of Tower Grove Park. She was 109 years old when I interviewed her, and was by far the oldest person I interviewed. The youngest was Milo Marston, who was born in 2008, 101 years after Dorothy Hunter. Milo also lives in the 3800 block of Connecticut, just a few doors from where Hunter grew up. The chance that would have in a town this big? One in a million? But this is a one in a million book.

Milo Marston stands in front of Dorothy Hunter's old house, holding a photo of Dorothy Hunter and her two siblings when they were kids. Dorothy is at the left. Milo, the youngest of those interviewed, lives a few doors from the childhood home of Hunter, the oldest of those interviewed.

Photo Credits

Amanda Doyle: 152 (bottom right), 168, 177

Annemarie Nauert: 136 (second from top right), 148

Beth Johnston: 40

Cameron Collins: 14 (second from bottom left), 25, 116 (bottom)

Cora (French) Katzen: 60 (middle left), 67 (top)

Darrell Fuse: 72

Darren Seals: 128

Darren Snow: 73

David Brendel, 82 (top right), 92

Discogs: 95 (top)

Don Korte: 35 (top), 41, 152 (top right)

Dorothy (Danner) Hunter: xiv (second from top right), 13

Florida Cargill: 60 (middle right), 66

Fred Blumenthal: 71

Gary and Robbie Raker: 28 (top right), 36

Greg Rhomberg: 13 (bottom), 95 (bottom)

James Conway: 51

Jim Merkel: 28 (bottom right), 34, 93, 94, 99, 100, 122 (second from top right), 131, 136 (top left), 144, 146, 150, 152 (top left), 166

John Burns: 60 (bottom middle), 75 (top left)

Joseph Sedberry: 136 (bottom left), 143

Joseph Winkler: 82 (bottom middle), 89, 173

Joyce Waskow: 104 (second from bottom left), 118

Kristin (Woehr) du Bruyn: 147

Kurt Walker: 104 (top left), 119

Library of Congress: xiv (bottom middle), 11, 50, 82 (bottom left), 90

Madelyn (Pedrotti) Gaasch family: 14 (top left), 23

Magic House: 152 (second from top right)

Marsha Vedova: 152 (second from bottom right), 162 (top)

Michael Hennon: 60 (top left), 77

Missouri Historical Society: xiv (top left, top right, second from top left, bottom left), 5, 6 (top), 7, 14 (top middle, second from top right, second from bottom right, bottom left), 28 (top left, second from top left, middle), 44 (all), 56, 58, 60 (top middle, top right, bottom left), 69 (top), 74, 82 (middle left, middle right), 87, 102 (bottom), 104 (second from top left, second from top right, bottom left, bottom right), 122 (second from bottom right), 159

Norman Plant: 82 (bottom right), 101

Pixabay: 24, 28 (bottom left), 37, 49, 54, 82 (top left), 88, 110, 114 (bottom), 122 (top right, second from bottom left), 127, 136 (bottom right), 141, 145, 163 (bottom), 165, 167

Ray Steinnerd: xiv (second from bottom right), 10 (bottom)

Saint Louis Zoo: 60 (bottom right), 79 (top)

Sidney Duerr family: 43

St. Louis Post-Dispatch: xiv (second from bottom left), 9, 12

State Historical Society of Missouri: 14 (top right), 19

Tabitha Stowers: 152 (bottom left), 163 (top)

Unsplash: 161

Valerie Shremp Hahn: 122 (top left), 129

Wikimedia Commons: xiv (bottom right, via State Library of Queensland, Australia), 10 (top, via State Library of Queensland, Australia), 21, 26 (top, via AlbertHerring), 33 (via L1327M), 35 (bottom), 52 (via Rudolph89), 55, 65 (via Pingsjong), 68, 69 (bottom, via Roger McLassus), 75 (bottom, via Auckland Museum), 79 (bottom), 91 (via Dwayne Pounds), 99, 102 (top), 104 (top right, via OREA2000), 111 (via OREA2000), 114 (top), 117 (via Chris Hagerman), 122 (bottom right), 133 (top, via Bill Bertram), 133 (bottom, via Dub), 135 (via Doug Coldwell), 136 (top right, via Jon DeJong), 149 (via RickDikeman), 152 (second from top left, via Wally Gobetz), 160 (via Wally Gobetz)

Sources

Introduction

Loftus, Elizabeth, telephone interview, December 26, 2018.

UCI Law website, Elizabeth F. Loftus, Distinguished Professor of Psychological Science and Law, https://www.law.uci.edu/faculty/full-time/loftus; Accessed December 31, 2018.

Encyclopaedia Britannica, Oliver North, United States Military Officer, https://www.britannica.com/biography/Oliver-North; Accessed undetermined date.

History: 2006: Duke lacrosse team suspended following sexual assault allegations, https://www.history.com/this-day-in-history/duke-lacrosse-team-suspended-following-sexual-assault-allegations; Accessed December 31, 2018.

Hope for a New Century, 1900–1919

Achievements in Public Health, 1900-1999: Healthier Mothers and Babies, CDC, *MMWR Weekly*, https://www.cdc.gov/mmwr/preview/mmwrhtml/mm4838a2.htm; Accessed April 18, 2018 and May 5, 2018.

Ancestry Popular Toys in History: What Your Ancestors Played With, https://blogs.ancestry.com/cm/popular-toys-in-history-what-your-ancestors-played-with; Accessed August 12, 2019.

Baker, Josephine, and Joyce Bouilon, *Josephine*, Boston: Da Capo Press, 1995.

Collins, Cameron, *Lost Treasures* of St. Louis, St. Louis: Reedy Press, 2017.

Downtown STL, Annie Malone Children and Family Services May Day Parade, https://downtownstl.org/event/annie-malone-may-day-parade-3/; Accessed August 12, 2019.

Farmers Almanac, Popular Christmas Gifts since 1900, https://www.farmersalmanac.com/popular-christmas-toys-since-1900-25956; Accessed August 12, 2019.

"Forgotten Lessons from the East St. Louis Race Riots," by Tony Rehagen, St. Louis Magazine, http://projects.stlmag.com/1917-stl-race-riots; Accessed May 26, 2018.

Gilbert, James, *Whose Fair? Experience, Memory, and the History of the Great St. Louis Exposition*, University of Chicago Press, Chicago, 2009.

Going to the Movies: Early Audiences, http://www.blackwellpublishing.com/content/bpl_images/content_store/sample_chapter/9780631219590/001.pdf; Accessed May 24, 2018.

Hahn, Emily *Times and Places*, New York: Thomas Y. Crowell Company, 1969.

Hunter, (Danner) Dorothy, interview, March 24, 2017.

Infoplease.com, U.S. History Timeline: Progressive Era and World Wars 1900-1949, https://www.infoplease.com/history/us/us-history-progressive-era-and-world-wars-1900-1949.

Legacy.com Dorothy Julia Banner Hunter obituary, https://www.legacy.com/obituaries/stltoday/obituary.aspx?n=dorothy-julia-hunter&pid=186789542; Accessed March 11, 2019.

Forty-Eighth Annual Report of the Board of Education of the City of St. Louis, Mo. for the Year Ending June 30, 1902, St. Louis: Nixon-Jones Printing Co., 1903.

Marion, Wenzel, *My Dad's St. Louis Boyhood: German Immigrants' Life, 1900-1915: Including Visits to the Louisiana Purchase Exposition*, Apple Valley, California: Wenzel Press, 2000.

Newsday Top Toys of the Decade: 1900 through today, https://www.newsday.com/lifestyle/family/top-toys-of-the-decade-1900-through-today-1.11251451; Accessed August 12, 2019.

A Preservation Plan for St. Louis Part I: Historic Contexts, The African-American Experience, City of St. Louis, https://www.stlouis-mo.gov/government/departments/planning/cultural-resources/preservation-plan/Part-I-African-American-Experience.cfm; Accessed May 26 and May 30, 2018.

Primm, James Neal, *Lion of the Valley 1764-1980*, 1st Edition, St. Louis: Missouri Historical Society Press, 1988.

Riley, Calvin, interview, August 12, 2019.

Shepley, Carol Ferring, *St. Louis: An Illustrated Timeline*, 2nd Edition, St. Louis: Reedy Press, 2018.

Sonderman, Joe, *St. Louis World's Fair 365*, St. Louis: Stellar Press, 2004.

The State Historical Society of Missouri, Historic Missourians: Annie Turnbo Malone (1869-1957), https://historicmissourians.shsmo.org/historicmissourians/name/m/malone/; Accessed August 12, 2019.

St. Louis Public Radio, The 109th Annie Malone May Day Parade Steps into Town, https://news.stlpublicradio.org/post/109th-annie-malone-may-day-parade-steps-town#stream/0; Accessed August 12, 2019.

St. Louis Post-Dispatch, December 31, 1899, January 1, 1900, January 2, 1900, January 3, 1900, January 4, 1900, January 5, 1900, July 18, 1902, January 29, 1903, May 27, 1906, June 13, 1907, November 21, 1907, November 23, 1907, March 20, 1908, September 15, 1908, September 21, 1908. June 13, 1910, November 12, 1911, July 28, 1913, February 15, 1914, July 11, 1915, October 6, 1915, June 8, 1919, June 18, 1919, July 4, 1916, December 22, 1918, June 8, 1919, October 7, 1919, June 6, 1948.

St. Louis Republic, January 5, 1900.

"The Story of Segregation in St. Louis," by Jeannette Cooperman, *St. Louis Magazine*, October 17, 2014, https://www.stlmag.com/news/the-color-line-race-in-st.-louis/; Accessed May 26, 2018.

Between the War and the Crash 1920–1929

African-American life during the Great Depression and the New Deal, https://www.britannica.com/topic/African-American/African-American-life-during-the-Great-Depression-and-the-New-Deal Accessed August 6, 2018.

Alamy Cowboys 1920s, Stock Photos and Images, https://www.alamy.com/stock-photo/cowboy-1920s.html; Accessed August 12, 2019.

Arbogast, Helen, interview, March 16, 2016.

Baseball Almanac, http://www.baseball-almanac.com/; Accessed July 13, 2018.

Collins, Cameron, *Lost Treasures of St. Louis*, St. Louis: Reedy Press, 2017.

CPI Inflation Calculator, http://www.in2013dollars.com/us/inflation/1923?amount=87400000; Accessed March 4, 2019.

Fontana, Frank, interview, August 22, 2018, and follow-up conversations.

Gaasch, Madeline, interview, November 22, 2017.

Hetzer, Ed, interview, February 9, 2018

Hotchner, *A.E. King of the Hill: A Memoir*, 1972, Harper & Row, New York.1972.

Jimerson, Louise, interview, November 2017.

Infoplease.com, U.S. History Timeline: Progressive Era and World Wars 1900-1949, https://www.infoplease.com/history/us/us-history-progressive-era-and-world-wars-1900-1949.

Meyer, Elizabeth Louise (Fresenburg), interview, undetermined date.

Primm, James Neal, *Lion of the Valley: St. Louis, Missouri, 1764-1980*, St. Louis: Pruitt Publishing Co., 1981.

Naslund, Ralph, interview, April 28, 2017.

Ott, Hortense "Blondie" (Bushman), interview, May 26, 2017, and follow-ups.

Riley, Calvin, interview, August 12, 2019.

St. Louis Post-Dispatch, October 4, 1922, November 17, 1923, December 9, 1954, March 30, 1926, October 11, 1926, May 21, 1927, June 19, 1927, June 20, 1927, October 2, 1927, October 5, 1927, December 23, 1929, November 17, 1923, December 9, 1954, November 1, 1986, September 30, 2016. June 21, 2009.

St. Louis Star, March 1, 1922, October 21, 1926, October 6, 1927, January 16, 1929, December 24, 1929, December 26, 1929.

Shepley, Carol Ferring, *St. Louis: An Illustrated Timeline*, 2nd Edition, St. Louis: Reedy Press, 2018.

Sixty-Seventh Annual Report of the Board of Education of the City of St. Louis, Mo. for the Year Ending June 21, 1921, St. Louis: St. Louis Board of Education, 1922.

What Do We Do All Day?: Classic Children's Books by the Decade: 1920s, https://www.whatdowedoallday.com/classic-childrens-books-by-the-decade-1920s-the-childrens-bookshelf/

Whitaker, Margaret, interview, March 29, 2017.

YouTube: 1927 - The Jazz Singer, https://www.youtube.com/watch?v=UYOY8dkhTpU; Accessed March 2, 2019.

AL JOLSON - "SWANEE" from Rhapsody in Blue WIDESCREEN -HD 1945, https://www.youtube.com/watch?v=bPmBPvHzF2c; Accessed March 2, 2019.

Louise Jimerson obituary, http://www.legacy.com/obituaries/belleville/obituary.aspx?n=louise-b-jimerson&pid=187871674&fhid=12523. http://www.bnd.com/living/magazine/article155178169.html

Primm, James Neal, *Lion of the Valley, 1764-1980*, 1st Edition, St. Louis: Missouri Historical Society Press, 1988.

The Roaring '20s for Kids, https://roaring20s.mrdonn.org/; Accessed March 2, 2019.

100 Greatest Songs of the 1920s. https://digitaldreamdoor.com/pages/best_songs-1920s.html; Accessed March 2, 2019.

Riley, Calvin, interview, August 12, 2019.

St. Louis Media History Foundation website, http://www.stlmediahistory.com/Radio/CallLetters. Accessed June 28, 2018.

Charles Lindbergh: An American Aviator, The Spirit of St. Louis Story. http://www.charleslindbergh.com/hall/spirit.asp; Accessed July 13, 2018/

Seventy-Ninth Annual Report of the Board of Education of the City of St. Louis, Missouri, for the Year Ending June 30, 1933.

Shepley, Carol Ferring, *St. Louis: An Illustrated Timeline*, 2nd Edition, St. Louis: Reedy Press, 2018.

Stock Market Crash of 1929, https://www.history.com/topics/1929-stock-market-crash; Accessed July 7, 2018.

Williams, Kenneth I. Williams, Trends in Child Dependency in St. Louis, 1860-1944, Research Bureau Social Planning Council of St. Louis and St. Louis County St. Louis, 1946.

1920-30.com, http://www.1920-30.com/toys/; Accessed July 16, 2018.

History of the ARC, https://www.thearc.org/who-we-are/history/name-change; Accessed July 16, 2018.

St. Louis Star, September 30, 1925, 1920-30.Com, http://www.1920-30.com/medicine/; Accessed July 16, 2018.

Darst, Katharine, St. Louis in the Twenties: The Girls Kept Their Shoes On, Missouri Historical Society Bulletin, October 1957.

Adams, Bea, The Decade That Roared, St. Louis Commerce, December 1984.

Hitting Bottom 1930–1939

Black Past, The Ville (St. Louis, Mo.), September 5, 2008, https://www.blackpast.org/uncategorized/ville/; Accessed August 13, 2019.

Brother, Can You Spare a Dime? https://www.youtube.com/watch?v=FIuSTT277XI; Accessed April 22, 2019.

Built St. Louis, Recalled to Life, Historic Downtown, Kiel Auditorium and Opera House, https://www.builtstlouis.net/opera.html; Accessed August 14, 2018.

Collins, Cameron, *Lost Treasures of St. Louis*, St. Louis: Reedy Press, 2017.

Crittenden, Jennie (Patania), interview, April 7, 2017.

C-SPAN. "How Americans First Learned of Pearl Harbor," https://www.c-span.org/video/?c546075/clip-americans-learned-pearl-harbor; Accessed August 19, 2018.

Danforth, William H., interview, July 5, 2017.

Digital History: "Children and the Great Depression," http://www.digitalhistory.uh.edu/active_learning/explorations/children_depression/depression_children_menu.cfm; Accessed August 12, 2019

Duerr, Sidney, interview, November 14, 2017, with numerous follow-ups.

Fontana, Frank, interview, August 22, 2018, and follow-up conversations.

Infoplease.com, U.S. History Timeline: Progressive Era and World Wars 1940-1949, https://www.infoplease.com/history/us/us-history-progressive-era-and-world-wars-1900-1949.

Naslund, Ralph, interview, April 28, 2017.

Harper, Elizabeth June, interview, June 15, 2017.

Hotchner, A.E. *King of the Hill: A Memoir*, New York: Harper & Row, 1972.

Jimerson, Louise, interview, November 2017.

Karras, Frieda Tsichlis, interview, August 23, 2018.

"Look Back 250: Great Depression Settles Hard on St. Louis," by Tim O'Neil, October 25, 2014, https://www.stltoday.com/news/local/govt-and-politics/look-back-great-depression-settles-hard-on-st-louis/article_59f9adc1-12b4-50dc-b136-7dfd3993cea1.html; Accessed April 16, 2019, and July 12, 2019.

McFerren, Dorothy, interview, August 8, 2017.

Missouri Historical Society, July 26, 2017, "St. Louis in the Great Depression," by Amanda Claunch, http://mohistory.org/blog/st-louis-in-the-great-depression/; Accessed July 25, 2018; http://great-depression-facts.com/; Accessed Aug. 1, 2018.

Old Time Radio: Children's Radio Shows, https://www.otrcat.com/childrens-radio-shows; Accessed August 12, 2019.

Primm, James Neal, *Lion of the Valley 1764-1980*, 1st Edition, St. Louis: Missouri Historical Society Press, 1988.

Raker, Marjorie (Jones), interview, October 13, 2017.

Riley, Calvin, interview, August 12, 2019.

Rodriguez, Manuel, "My 1930s Education at the Movies, The Golden Age of Hollywood Taught Me About War, Crime, Natural Disasters—and What was Funny About America," http://www.whatitmeanstobeamerican.org/encounters/my-1930s-education-at-the-movies/; Accessed August 13, 2018.

Schuette, Mary, interview, February 16, 2018.

St. Louis City Talk, February 14, 2010, The Ville neighborhood, http://www.stlouiscitytalk.com/posts/2010/02/ville-neighborhood; Accessed February 14, 2010.

St. Louis Post-Dispatch, various dates during the 1930s, and November 28, 2012.

St. Louis Star, St. Louis Star and Times, and *St. Louis Star-Times*. Various dates during the 1930s.

St. Louis Walk of Fame, A.E. Hotchner, http://www.stlouiswalkoffame.org/inductees/ae-hotchner.htm; Accessed August 9, 2018.

Tsichlis, George, Oral History interview with George P. Tsichlis concerning the Early Greek Community in St. Louis and the Great Depression, conducted July 28, 1974. Interviewer: Steven Peter Tsichlis. Transcribed by Michael G. Tsichlis, PhD.

Tsichlis, Dr. Michael, interviews, various times in July and August 2018.

The Ville Historic District, https://www.stlouis-mo.gov/government/departments/planning/cultural-resources/The-Ville-Historic-District.cfm; Accessed August 13, 2019.

Zwick, Vivian (Wides), interview, August 24, 2017, with follow-ups.

From Rations to Plenty 1940–1949

Baseball Reference: 1946 St. Louis Cardinals Roster (40 Man) https://www.baseball-reference.com/teams/STL/1946-roster.shtml; Accessed September 16, 2018.

Brown, Ellis II, interview, undetermined date.

Collins, Cameron, *Lost Treasures of St. Louis*, St. Louis: Reedy Press, 2017.

Conway, James, interview, around December 2017.

C-SPAN. "How Americans First Learned of Pearl Harbor," https://www.c-span.org/video/?c546075/clip-americans-learned-pearl-harbor; Accessed August 19, 2018.

Danforth, William H., interview, July 5, 2017.

Falkenberg, Betty (Cole), interview, October 4, 2017.

Hannibal, Betty (Emery), interview, June 22, 2017.

Harper, Elizabeth June, interview, June 15, 2017.

Hartke, Paul, interview, May 12, 2017.

Head, Claretta, interview, March 28, 2017.

History: V-J Day, https://www.history.com/topics/world-war-ii/v-j-day; Accessed August 28, 2018.

Infoplease.com, U.S. History Timeline: Progressive Era and World Wars 1940-1949, https://www.infoplease.com/history/us/us-history-progressive-era-and-world-wars-1900-1949.

Missouri Historical Review, published by State Historical Society of Missouri, April 1943, July 1943, January 1944, April 1944, July 1944, October 1944, January 1945, April 1945, July 1945.

News of St. Louis Hills, May 1946, October, 1946, November 1946, January 1948, April 1948, May 1948, November 1948, December 1948, January 1949, April 1949.

Official Manual: State of Missouri, 1973-1974, The Role of the Negro in Missouri History, Civil Rights, 1940-1970, https://law.wustl.edu/staff/taylor/manual/civrits.htm; Accessed September 14, 2018.

Olds, Edward,Trends in Child Dependency in St. Louis, 1860-1944, for Research Bureau, Social Planning Council of St. Louis and St. Louis Council.

The People's History 1940s Popular Vintage Children's Toys with Prices, Descriptions and Images http://www.thepeoplehistory.com/40stoys.html; Accessed September 15, 2018.

Play Stuff Blog, The Home Front: Toy Production During World War II.

History on the Net: What Happened After the Attack on Pearl Harbor, https://www.historyonthenet.com/what-happened-after-the-attack-of-pearl-harbor/; Accessed August 19, 2018.

Pearl Harbor 1941: Japan Attacks United States, https://www.nola.com/military/index.ssf/2013/12/pearl_harbor_1941_japan_attack.html; Accessed August 19. 2018.

Primm, James Neal, *Lion of the Valley 1764-1980*, 1st Edition, St. Louis: Missouri Historical Society Press, 1988.

Ranker: The Best '40s Kids Movies, https://www.ranker.com/list/best-40s-kids-movies/ranker-film; Accessed September 15, 2018.

Riley, Calvin, interview, August 12, 2019.

Schriedel, Gerald, interview, undetermined date.

Shepley, Carol Ferring, *St. Louis: An Illustrated Timeline*, 2nd Edition, St. Louis: Reedy Press, 2018.

St. Louis Board of Education Yearbook 1943 or '44 about daycare facilities for children of working moms.

St. Louis Cardinals Timeline 1940s, http://stlouis.cardinals.mlb.com/stl/historyeline.jsp; Accessed September 16, 2018.

St. Louis Globe-Democrat, December 7, 1941, December 8, 1941.

St. Louis Post-Dispatch, September 21, 1941, December 7, 1941, December 8, 1941, January 16, 1944, December 31, 1945, January 2, 1946, February 11, 2016, September 6, 2017.

St. Louis Star-Times, December 8, 1941, March 15, 1947.

Stevens, David, interview, April 20, 2017.

Webster-Kirkwood Times, May 5, 2017.

Williams, Kenneth I. Williams, Trends in Child Dependency in St. Louis, 1860-1944, Research Bureau Social Planning Council of St. Louis and St. Louis County St. Louis, 1946. https://www.prb.org/justhowmanybabyboomersarethere/; Accessed September 16, 2018.

Beaver's Decade 1950–1959

Amazon Original Free Meek, Elvis Presley Movies, https://www.imdb.com/list/ls059414601/; Accessed August 14, 2019.

Backhaus, Harriet, interview, October 2017.

Blumenthal, Fred, interview, March 25, 2017.

Burns, John, interview, September 18, 2017, speech, March 31, 2019.

Cargill, Florida, interview, undetermined date.

Collins, Cameron, *Lost Treasures of St. Louis*, St. Louis: Reedy Press, 2017.

Cowan, Jack, interview, various times.

"FBI: A Byte Out of History: The Bobby Greenlease Kidnapping," https://www.fbi.gov/news/stories/a-byte-out-of-history-the-bobby-greenlease-kidnapping1; Accessed May 30, 2019.

Farmer, Holly, interview, April 7, 2017.

Fuse, Darrell, interview, October 2017, speech, March 31, 2019.

Gebhardt, Shirley (Kubina), interview, September 23, 2017.

Hennon, Michael, speech, March 31, 2019, and interview at undetermined time.

Horne, James, interview, April 8, 2017.

Infoplease.com, Timeline: Mid-Century and Cold War, 1950-1999, https://www.infoplease.com/history/us/us-history-mid-century-and-cold-war-1950-1999.

Jenkins, Eric, interview, July 31, 2017.

Katzen, Cora, interview, October 7, 2017.

McDonalds Original Menu, https://www.pinterest.com/pin/447686019177986594/; Accessed August 15, 2019.

Mueller, Robert (Bob), C. interview, undetermined date.

100 Greatest Rock ‘n’ Roll Artists of the ’50s, https://digitaldreamdoor.com/pages/best_artists50s.html; Accessed August 14, 2019.

Primm, James Neal, *Lion of the Valley 1764-1980*, 1st Edition, St. Louis, Missouri: Missouri Historical Society Press, 1988.

Riley, Calvin, interview, August 12, 2019.

Schroeder, Mary (Kubiak), interview, November 2017.

Shepley, Carol Ferring, *St. Louis: An Illustrated Timeline*, 2nd Edition, St. Louis: Reedy Press, 2018.

Smith, Monroe Jr., interview, November 1, 2017, and speech, March 31, 2019.

Tegethoff, Lois, interview, October 7, 2017.

Walker, Margaret (Tinius), interview, June 30, 2017, with follow-up questions.

Paiewonsky, (Jones) Lolita, interview, October 28, 2017.

Hope Dashed 1960–1969

All Music Bob Kuban: Artist Biography by Eugene Chadbourne, https://www.allmusic.com/artist/bob-kuban-mn0001467617/biography; Accessed August 21, 2019.

Baseball-Reference.com, St. Louis Cardinals Team History & Encyclopedia, https://www.baseball-reference.com/teams/STL/index.shtml; Accessed September 19, 2019.

BND, Two men claim to be Johnny Rabbitt. Who was your favorite? https://www.bnd.com/living/liv-columns-blogs/answer-man/article177908741.html; Accessed November 6, 2018.

Brendel, Dave, interview, October 7, 2017.

Butler, Anthony “Tony,” interview, October 7, 2017.

Collins, Cameron, *Lost Treasures of St. Louis*, St. Louis: Reedy Press, 2017.

Cusumano, Frank, interview, June 23, 2017, with follow-up correspondence.

"The Day We Said Good Bye: A Look Back At Iconic Moments From Busch Stadium II." https://www.stltoday.com/sports/baseball/professional/the-day-we-said-goodbye-a-look-back-at-iconic/collection_502a3ad6-5dc2-54c1-a201-4efb4ab22336.html#1; Accessed September 19, 2019.

ESPN, MLB Team History ESPN, MLB Team History - St. Louis Cardinals Season Results, http://www.espn.com/mlb/history/teams/_/team/stl; Accessed November 3, 2018.

St. Louis Cardinals Season Results, http://www.espn.com/mlb/history/teams/_/team/stl; Accessed November 3, 2018.

"Fifty Years Ago This Month, The Beatles Played Their Only St. Louis Show," https://www.riverfronttimes.com/stlouis/the-concert-from-hell/Content?oid=3089250&showFullText=true; Accessed August 21, 2019.

Fort, Gary, interview, October 14, 2017.

Gurney, Linda (Seiferth), interview, October 7, 2017, and speech, March 31, 2019.

Infoplease.com Timeline: Mid-Century and Cold War, 1950-1999, https://www.infoplease.com/history/us/us-history-mid-century-and-cold-war-1950-1999.

Kinealy, Dennis, interview, October 14, 2017.

Heinzerling, Antonina (Giardina), interview, May 25, 2017.

History, Art and Archives, United States House of Representatives, Clay, William Lacy Sr., https://history.house.gov/People/Detail/11058; Accessed August 15, 2019.

History of Parkway School District, Factsheet provided by Paul Tandy, Chief Communications & Emergency Management Officer, Parkway School District. https://www.jfklibrary.org/learn/about-jfk/life-of-john-f-kennedy/fast-facts-john-f-kennedy/high-hopes; Accessed about October 31, 2018.

Holleman, Joe, interview, February 14, 2019, with follow-ups.

La Croix, Colleen, interview, October 21, 2017, speech March 31, 2019.

Levy, Sterling, interview, May 30, 2017.

Lesher, Jeff, interview, May 18, 2017.

Lindbergh Schools history provided by Beth Johnston, district chief communications officer.

McGee, Gregg, interview, October 17, 2018, with follow-up.

Nelson, Jane, interview, July 15, 2017, and speech, March 31, 2019.

Official Manual, State of Missouri, 1973-1974 The Role of the Negro in Missouri History, https://law.wustl.edu/staff/taylor/manual/civrits.htm; Accessed November 8, 2018.

St. Louis Blues Team History, https://sportsteamhistory.com/st-louis-blues; Accessed November 3, 2018.

Population of St. Louis City and County, and Missouri 1820-2010, Saint Louis Population figures from the U.S. Census Bureau. https://www.genealogybranches.com/stlouispopulation.html; Accessed November 8, 2018 and January 9, 2019.

Primm, James Neal, *Lion of the Valley 1764-1980*, 1st Edition, St. Louis: Missouri Historical Society Press 1988.

Quinn, Michael, interview, April 7, 2017.

Riley, Calvin, interview, August 12, 2019.

St. Louis Hawks http://www.sportsecyclopedia.com/nba/stlhawks/stlhawks.html; Accessed September 19, 2019, Sports Team History, St. Louis Cardinals (Football) Team History Sports Team History, https://sportsteamhistory.com/st-louis-cardinals-az; Accessed November 3, 2018.

St. Louis Media History Foundation, KSHE Station History, http://www.stlmediahistory.org/index.php/Radio/RadioArticles/kshe-station-history; Accessed Nov. 6, 2018.

St. Louis Local Kid Shows, http://www.tvparty.com/lostst.html; Accessed November 7, 2018.

http://projects.stlmag.com/the-history-of-protests-in-st-louis; Accessed November 11, 2018.

St. Louis Post-Dispatch, February 22, 1960, January 18, 1968, February 20, 1968, April 5, 1968 April 8, 1968, July 19, 2018.

Shepley, Carol Ferring, *St. Louis: An Illustrated Timeline*, 2nd Edition, St. Louis: Reedy Press, 2018.

Smith, Perkins, interview, October 28, 2017.

Sohm, Joseph, interview, August 2017.

Taylor, Joseph, interview, August 2019.

Winkler, Joseph, various interviews, 2017-2019.

Wolf, Tom, interview, October 7, 2017.

Yoffie, Joseph, interview, June 19, 2017.

What's Going On? 1970–1979

Hrabosky: The Mad Hungarian, http://www.alhrabosky.com/; Accessed February 16, 2019.

Billboard: The 35 Best Disco Songs Ever, https://www.billboard.com/photos/7445749/best-disco-tracks-of-all-time-dance-music; Accessed January 10, 2019.

Child Trends: Birthday to Unmarried Women, https://www.childtrends.org/indicators/births-to-unmarried-women; Accessed January 27, 28, and 29, 2019.

Children's Hospital of Philadelphia, Vaccine History: Development by Year, https://www.chop.edu/centers-programs/vaccine-education-center/vaccine-history/developments-by-year; Accessed August 15, 2019.

Coldwater Creek Facts, http://www.coldwatercreekfacts.com/; Accessed August 6, 2019.

Collins, Cameron, *Lost Treasures of St. Louis*, St. Louis: Reedy Press, 2017.

Duncan, Jonathan, interview, February 13, 2019, with follow-ups.

EH.net, African Americans in the Twentieth Century, https://eh.net/encyclopedia/african-americans-in-the-twentieth-century/; Accessed August 15, 2019.

Epstein, Scott, interview, October 14, 2017.

Fusco, Sharon (Schiller), interview, May 24, 2017.

Hayden, John, interview for *West End World*, January 5, 2018.

Huffington Post, "Reasons for the Surge in Birth to Single Women," by Nigel Barber, https://www.huffingtonpost.com/nigel-barber/reasons-for-the-surge-in-_b_3831174.html; Accessed January 29, 2019.

Holleman, Joe, interview, February 14, 2019, with follow-ups.

IFS (Institute for Family Studies). How We Ended Up With by Forty Percent of Children Born Out of Wedlock, by Robert VerBruggen.

IMDb: The Best 70s Teen Movie, https://www.imdb.com/list/ls022867265/; Accessed January 16, 2019.

https://ifstudies.org/blog/how-we-ended-up-with-40-percent-of-children-born-out-of-wedlock; Accessed January 29, 2019.

Infoplease.com, Timeline: Mid-Century and Cold War 1950-1999, https://www.infoplease.com/history/us/us-history-mid-century-and-cold-war-1950-1999.

Kinealy, Dennis, interview, October 14, 2017.

Lesher, Jeff, interview, May 18, 2017.

"Looking back at the glory days of the Mississippi River Festival," *Stltoday*, June 17, 2018, https://www.stltoday.com/news/archives/looking-back-at-the-glory-days-of-the-mississippi-river/collection_8180e33b-cc6c-5224-98f7-f93aa1505595.html; Accessed January 5, 2019.

Led Zeppelin Setlist at St. Louis Arena, St. Louis, MO, USA, Tour: North American Tour 1975, https://www.setlist.fm/setlist/led-zeppelin/1975/st-louis-arena-st-louis-mo-3bd600c0.html; Accessed January 5, 2019.

Merkel, James (Jim) Patrick, interview, April 27, 2017.

Missouri Census Data Center, Missouri City Population 1900-1990, http://mcdc.missouri.edu/trends/historical/cities1900-1990.pdf; Accessed January 11 and 28, 2019.

National Baseball Hall of Fame: Bob Gibson Becomes the Second Pitcher to Record 3,000 Strikeouts, https://baseballhall.org/discover/bob-gibson-throws-3000th-strikeout; Accessed February 16, 2019.

Nelson, Jane (Dibble), interview, July 15, 2017, and speech.

Office of the Historian, Department of State, The Iranian Hostage Crisis, https://history.state.gov/departmenthistory/short-history/iraniancrises; Accessed January 9, 2019.

The People History: 1970s Popular Vintage Children's Toys with Prices, Descriptions and Images, http://www.thepeoplehistory.com/70stoys.html; Accessed January 16, 2019.

Primm, James Neal, *Lion of the Valley 1764-1980*, 1st Edition, St. Louis: Missouri Historical Society Press, 1988.

Ranker: Best '70s Cartoons, https://www.ranker.com/list/best-70s-cartoons/ranker-tv; Accessed January 16, 2019.

Ranker: Best '70s Movies, https://www.ranker.com/list/best-70s-kids-movies/ranker-film; Accessed Jan. 16, 2019.

Real Clear Religion: When Evangelicals Were Cool, https://www.realclearreligion.org/articles/2012/07/09/when_evangelicals_were_cool.html; Accessed January 7, 2019.

Riley, Calvin, interview, August 12, 2019.

St. Louis Post-Dispatch, May 5, 1970. *Post-Dispatch*, December 9, 1973, January 2, 1977. January 3, 1977. *St. Louis Post-Dispatch*, February 27, 1977, April 7, 1979.

SetlistFM The Setlist Wiki, Mississippi River Festival Setlists, https://www.setlist.fm/festivals/mississippi-river-festival-13d6adf1.html; Accessed January 10, 2019.

Shaw, Susan (Waskow), interview, February 2018.

Shepley, Carol Ferring, *St. Louis: An Illustrated Timeline*, 2nd Edition, St. Louis: Reedy Press, 2018.

Song Facts Song Writing: Jesus in Pop Hits: The Gospel Songs That Went Mainstream. https://www.songfacts.com/blog/writing/jesus-in-pop-hits-the-gospel-songs-that-went-mainstream; Accessed January 7, 2019.

Spirits of St. Louis, http://www.remembertheaba.com/spirits-of-st-louis.html; Accessed February 16, 2019.

Still a thrill: Six Flags after 40 years https://www.stltoday.com/entertainment/still-a-thrill-six-flags-after-years/article_19337425-92e5-5f43-810d-d0cfd0f3294d.html; Accessed January 16, 2019.

Walker, Kurt, interview, early 2018, with speech, March 31, 2019.

Weidler, Jason, interview, November 29, 2017, with follow-ups.

Workman, Ann, interview, November 30, 2017, with speech, March 31, 2019.

World Population Review, St. Charles County, Missouri, Population 2018, http://worldpopulationreview.com/us-counties/mo/st-charles-county-population/; Accessed January 11, 2019.

Young, Melanie, interview, undetermined date.

The Reagan Years, 1980–1989

Appleby, Brenda, interview, May 15, 2017, with follow-ups.

Back to the Future, Part II, https://backtothefuture.fandom.com/wiki/Back_to_the_Future_Part_II; Accessed August 2, 2019.

Best Life. 20 Things Every "Cool Kid" Growing Up in the 1980s Owned, https://bestlifeonline.com/cool-kid-things-1980s/; Accessed August 2, 2019.

Cardinals All-Time Players, http://stlouis.cardinals.mlb.com/stl/history/players.jsp; Accessed August 2, 2019.

Collins, Cameron, *Lost Treasures of St. Louis*, St. Louis: Reedy Press, 2017.

Dairaghi, Kevin, interview, October 17, 2017, with follow-ups.

Duffin, Amanda (Tinnin), interview, November 25, 2019, with follow-ups.

Hahn, Valerie Schremp, interview, November 4, 2019, speech, March 31, 2019.

Hughes, Jennifer, interview, undetermined time, with follow-ups.

Infoplease.com, Timeline: Mid-Century and Cold War, 1950-1999, https://www.infoplease.com/history/us/us-history-mid-century-and-cold-war-1950-1999.

Kasel, Clayton, interview, undetermined date.

Maguire, David, interview, July 10, 2017.

Ranker: The Greatest Teen Movies of the 1980s, https://www.ranker.com/list/best-80s-teen-movies/ranker-film; Accessed August 2, 2019.

Riley, Calvin, interview, August 12, 2019.

Seals, Darren, interview, early 2019.

Shaw, Susan (Waskow), interview, February 2018.

Shepley, Carol Ferring, *St. Louis: An Illustrated Timeline*, 2nd Edition, St. Louis: Reedy Press, 2018.

Sports Team History, https://sportsteamhistory.com/st-louis-cardinals-az; Accessed August 2, 2019.

Star Trek Movies in Order, https://www.imdb.com/list/ls056782571/; Accessed August 2, 2019.

Wallace, Ramelle, interview, November 20, 2017, speech, March 31, 2019.

The Weirdest Parenting Advice We've Tried the Past 100 years, by Brie Dyas, March 13, 2017, https://www.goodhousekeeping.com/life/parenting/g4223/weird-parenting-trends-100-years/; Accessed August 15, 2019.

Into the Future, 1990–1999

Baraba, Sarah, interview, December 6, 2017.

Bustle: 10 Things We Genuinely Miss About '90s Internet, Because Nostalgia Runs Deep. https://www.bustle.com/articles/159061-10-things-we-genuinely-miss-about-90s-internet-because-nostalgia-runs-deep; Accessed August 3, 2019.

Characteristics of Children's Families 1: Household Family Structure: 1990-2000, https://www.census.gov/population/www/documentation/twps0078/maps0201.pdf; Accessed August 3, 2019.

Collins, Cameron, *Lost Treasures of St. Louis*, St. Louis: Reedy Press, 2017.

Dial-up Internet Connection exclusive, https://www.youtube.com/watch?v=UvoyYFOaoYQ; Accessed August 3, 2019.

Du Bruyn, Kristin (Woehr), interview, undetermined date in 2017 or 2018.

Dzidic, Andrej, undetermined date in 2017 or 2018.

EH.net, African Americans in the Twentieth Century, https://eh.net/encyclopedia/african-americans-in-the-twentieth-century/; Accessed August 15, 2019.

Encyclopedia Britannica, Y2K bug https://www.britannica.com/technology/Y2K-bug.; Accessed on undetermined date.

Encyclopedia Britannica: Television in the United States: The 1990s: The Loss of Shared Experiences, https://www.britannica.com/art/television-in-the-United-States/The-1990s-the-loss-of-shared-experience; Accessed August 4, 2019.

Guth, Peter, interview, October 2017.

Hayes, Madison, interview, June 5, 2017.

Infoplease.com, Timeline: Mid-Century and Cold War 1950-1999, https://www.infoplease.com/history/us/us-history-mid-century-and-cold-war-1950-1999.

Johnson, Andrea, interview, November 24, 2017, with follow-ups.

Maguire, David, interview, July 10, 2017, with follow-ups.

Marie Claire: The Best '90s Movies to Binge-Watch Right Now, https://www.marieclaire.com/culture/g22520389/best-90s-movies; Accessed August 4, 2019.

Martin, Jason, interview, June 21, 2017.

Nauert, Annemarie, interview, October 7, 2017, and follow-ups.

Mikow, Victoria (Vicki) Ann Tisset, interview, undetermined time, speech, March 31, 2019, and follow-ups.

Popular Mechanics: Whatever Happened to the V-Chip, https://www.popularmechanics.com/culture/tv/a19408909/20-years-ago-v-chip/; Accessed August 4, 2019.

Ranker: The Greatest Kids Movies of the 1990s, https://www.ranker.com/list/best-90s-kids-movies/ranker-film; Accessed August 15, 2019.

Riley, Calvin, interview, August 12, 2019.

Sedberry, Joseph, interview, March 10, 2018, with follow-ups.

Shepley, Carol Ferring, *St. Louis: An Illustrated Timeline*, 2nd Edition, St. Louis: Reedy Press, 2018.

Smith, Kiarra Lynn, interview, October 14, 2017.

Brave New World, 2000–2019

Attention-Deficit / Hyperactivity Disorder (ADHD), Centers for Disease Control and Prevention: National Prevalence of ADHD and Treatment: New statistics for children and adolescents, 2016, https://www.cdc.gov/ncbddd/adhd/features/national-prevalence-adhd-and-treatment.html; Accessed July 25, 2019.

Baraba, Sarah, interview, December 6, 2017.

Baseball Reference, St. Louis Cardinals Team History & Encyclopedia, St. Louis Cardinals Team History & Encyclopedia, https://www.baseball-reference.com/teams/STL/index.shtml; Accessed June 26, 2019.

Biography, Barack Obama. https://www.biography.com/us-president/barack-obama; Accessed September 19, 2019.

Biography, Donald Trump, https://www.biography.com/us-president/donald-trump, https://www.biography.com/us-president/donald-trump; Accessed September 19, 2019.

Collins, Cameron, *Lost Treasures of St. Louis*, St. Louis: Reedy Press, 2017.

Council on Contemporary Families: An Analysis of New Census Data on Family Structure, Education, and Income, https://docs.google.com/document/d/1uPJNDI6_rQDv4BWXQTxF8ajeKZ-_2b4Fj8P0y6e4eUA/edit; Accessed September 11, 2019.

Economic Policy Institute, 50 years after the Kerner Commission, https://docs.google.com/document/d/1a7EaxD7iRGq_0dI8otVNvsWJdUPnlibOYsgmDsuCa6A/edit#; Accessed August 20, 2019.

Facts and Trends: *Meet Generation Z*, by James Emery White, Book Review https://factsandtrends.net/2017/06/23/meet-generation-z-james-emery-white-book-review/

Forward Through Ferguson: A Path Toward Racial Equity, The Ferguson Commission Report, https://3680or2khmk3bzkp33juiea1-wpengine.netdna-ssl.com/wp-content/uploads/2015/09/101415_FergusonCommissionReport.pdf; Accessed September11, 2019.

George W. Bush, https://www.whitehouse.gov/about-the-white-house/presidents/george-w-bush/https://www.whitehouse.gov/about-the-white-house/presidents/george-w-bush/; Accessed September 19, 2019.

How to Schedule, Plan for, and Swap Regular Playdates, https://www.liveabout.com/scheduling-playdates-for-your-children-2997703; Accessed June 24, 2019.

Hughes, Jennifer, interview, undetermined time, with follow-ups.

La Croix, Aodhan, speech, March 31, 2019, and interview, November 2017, and follow-ups.

Kenner, Aurora, interview, November 4, 2017.

Lindbergh Schools: Board Approves No-Tax-Rate- Increase Bond Issue, https://go.lindberghschools.ws/site/default.aspx?PageType=3&DomainID=4&ModuleInstanceID=12349&ViewID=6446EE88-D30C-497E-9316-3F8874B3E108&RenderLoc=0&FlexDataID=35356&PageID=1; Accessed July 24, 2019.

Los Angeles Times, "African Americans are the only U.S. racial group earning less than in 2000," https://www.latimes.com/business/la-fi-african-american-income-20170915-story.html; Accessed August 13, 2019.

The Majority of Children Live with Two Parents, Census Bureau Reports. https://www.census.gov/newsroom/press-releases/2016/cb16-192.html, accessed January 14, 2020.

Market Watch: African-American college graduation rates hit all-time high, but economic outcomes lag, https://www.marketwatch.com/story/college-graduation-rates-for-african-americans-are-at-an-all-time-high-so-why-arent-their-finances-2018-03-01; Accessed August 20, 2019.

Missouri Charter Public School Association, St. Louis Charter Public School Directory, https://www.mocharterschools.org/apps/pages/index.jsp?uREC_ID=306930&type=d; Accessed June 26, 2019.

Missouri Department of Education Charter Schools, https://dese.mo.gov/quality-schools/charter-schools; Accessed June 26, 2019.

Millennial Outreach, Meet Generation Z - Book Summary, https://millennial-outreach.missionalmarketing.com/meet-generation-z-book-summary/; Accessed August 13, 2019.

Marston, Milo, interview, November 2, 2019.

Nelson, Gregory, speech, June 29, 2019.

New York Times, July 24, 2008. *New York Times*: "Supreme Court makes same-sex marriage a right nationwide," June 26, 2016, https://www.nytimes.com/2015/06/27/us/supreme-court-same-sex-marriage.html; Accessed September 11, 2019.

Pew Research Center, FactTank, Key facts about race and marriage, 50 years after *Loving v. Virginia*. https://www.pewresearch.org/fact-tank/2017/06/12/key-facts-about-race-and-marriage-50-years-after-loving-v-virginia/; Accessed August 13, 2019.

Pew Research Center, Teens, Social Media & Technology, Overview 2015, April 9, 2015 https://www.pewinternet.org/2015/04/09/teens-social-media-technology-2015/; Accessed August 14, 2019.

Pew Research Center: The Rise in Dual Income Households, https://www.pewresearch.org/ft_dual-income-households-1960-2012-2/; Accessed September 11, 2019.

Pittman, Treveon, interview, July 28, 2019.

The Project Gutenberg EBook of *The Tempest*, by William Shakespeare, https://www.gutenberg.org/files/23042/23042-h/23042-h.htm; Accessed September 17, 2019.

Riley, Calvin, interview, August 12, 2019.

St. Louis desegregation program headed for phase out, June 10, 2016, https://www.stltoday.com/news/local/education/st-louis-desegregation-program-headed-for-phase-out/article_9dadfa4c-3d49-5b80-b6ec-2b1c03d2e5c7.html; Accessed August 13, 2019.

St. Louis Post-Dispatch, August 20, 2019, August 21, 2019.

Shepley, Carol Ferring, *St. Louis: An Illustrated Timeline*, 2nd Edition, St. Louis: Reedy Press, 2018.

Smith, Kiarra Lynn, interview, October 14, 2017.

Stowers, Tabitha (Tabby), interview, January 20, 2018.

Ted Drewes Frozen Custard, Menu, https://www.ranker.com/list/best-90s-kids-movies/ranker-film; Accessed August 15, 2019.

Weighing School Backpacks, The New York Times, July 21, 2009.

White, James Emery, *Meet Generation Z: Understanding and Reaching the New Post-Christian World*, Grand Rapids, Michigan: Baker Books, 2017.

Vedova, Alison, interview, December 16, 2017.

Yanamadala, Vindhya, interview, October 2017.

Webster-Kirkwood Times, January 18, 2019.

Wifa, Waamene, interview, October 2017, with follow-up speech, March 31, 2019.

Epilogue

Cinema Treasures, Manchester Drive-In, 12610 Manchester Road, Des Peres, MO 63131, http://cinematreasures.org/theaters/19793/photos; Accessed December 31, 2018.

Jimmy Merkel kindergarten report card, 1956-57, by Gretchen L. Kilpatrick, teacher.

Missouri Department of Transportation 2016 St. Louis District Traffic Volume and Commercial Vehicle Count Map, https://www.modot.org/sites/default/files/documents/multimodal/2016_traffic_sl.pdf; Accessed December 31, 2018.

St. Louis Post-Dispatch, July 24, 1960.

Schmitt, Lois, various interviews at various times, 2017-2019.

Merkel, Charles, various interviews at various times, 2017-2019.

Index